THORNS & ROSES

THORNS & ROSES
NEIL KINNOCK
— Speeches 1983-1991 —
Introduced by Peter Kellner

HUTCHINSON
London

© The Labour Party 1983, 1984, 1985, 1986, 1987, 1988, 1989, 1990, 1991
© Introduction 1992 Peter Kellner

This edition first published in 1992 by
Hutchinson

Random Century Group Ltd
20 Vauxhall Bridge Road, London SW1V 2SA

Random Century Australia (Pty) Ltd
20 Alfred Street, Milsons Point, Sydney, NSW 2061, Australia

Random Century New Zealand Ltd
PO Box 40–086, Glenfield, Auckland 10, New Zealand

Random Century South Africa (Pty) Ltd
PO Box 337, Bergvlei, 2012, South Africa

A CIP catalogue record for this book is available
from the British Library

ISBN 0 09 177368 7

Photoset by Raven Typesetters, Ellesmere Port, South Wirral
Printed and bound in Great Britain by
Mackays of Chatham PLC, Chatham, Kent

CONTENTS

INTRODUCTION

During the Second World War, shortly before Japan attacked Pearl Harbor, one of President Roosevelt's aides visited London. After a series of intensive meetings he professed himself entirely satisfied with everything he had discovered – except for one thing. He remained mystified by the way Winston Churchill wrote his speeches. The President possessed a clutch of speech-writers, and occasionally said something memorable. Churchill, on the other hand, had no full-time speech-writers, and yet almost every month he said something that inspired his audience. What, the aide wondered, was the secret: who supplied Churchill with such haunting words?

'It's simple,' replied his British host. 'He rolls his own.'

These days there is probably not a single senior politician in the Western world who 'rolls his own'. Speech-writers, phrase-makers and diction-advisers abound. Journalists presented with an advance text of a leader's speech carrying the familiar injunction to 'check against delivery' seldom need to make many alterations.

Neil Kinnock comes nearer than most to providing an exception. He still refuses to read his speeches from the chest-high screens of sincerity machines. To the frequent dismay of television news producers, eager for short sound-bites, and the anxiety of his staff, worried lest he strays too far from some carefully constructed form of words, Kinnock treats the sheets of paper in front of him more as a final draft than a sacred text.

This approach has its problems, but also its benefits. The main drawback is that it tends to fuel the charge that Kinnock is a 'Welsh windbag'. In general, his conference speeches have seldom displayed the worst excesses: his prolixity has been more evident in interviews. But even his closest friends wince at his tendency to stretch a succinct statement into an elasticated tangle.

1

For example, in 1987, following Labour's heavy election defeat, Kinnock spoke of the importance of the party's policy review. According to the advance text distributed to journalists, this is how he intended to describe its basic aim:

> What we will be doing is developing the means to further the ends of democratic socialism: the commitments to community, to democracy, to justice, to real individual liberty that is not dependent upon the ability to pay . . .

When he delivered his speech, what he actually said was:

> What we will be doing in that process of review, and the activities related to that and many other campaigns, is to develop the means to further the ends of democratic socialism. We shall further the commitments to community, democracy and justice. And to real individual liberty that does not depend for its exercise on the ability of the individual to pay.

Kinnock had taken thirty-seven words and expanded them to sixty-two. Worse, he had introduced a rambling subordinate clause ('. . . and the activities related to that and many other campaigns . . .') that translated a piece of simple prose into a passage that was needlessly difficult for the casual listener to digest. In an earlier era, when important politicians made long and demanding speeches, such lapses would not have mattered. By William Gladstone's standards, Kinnock has always been a model of brevity. But modern politics, and today's media, demand different standards. Had Gladstone waged his Midlothian campaign in front of the television cameras without changing his style, he would doubtless have provoked complaints about 'tartan tedium'.

Yet against the drawback to Kinnock's style must be set the advantages. At his best, he refines his speeches to remarkable effect. When Labour gathered in Bournemouth at the end of September, 1985, friends, foes and journalists waited to see whether he would attack the Militant Tendency, and if so in what terms. Militant members, led by Derek Hatton, effectively controlled Liverpool City Council. Forty-eight hours before the Bournemouth conference opened, Hatton hired a fleet of taxis to send redundancy notices to all council employees. To Militant this was a consciousness-raising element of its strategy of confronting the Government. To almost everyone else it looked like the kind of casual, cynical extremism that was bound to give Labour a bad name.

On the morning of Tuesday, 1 October, the first people outside Kinnock's entourage were briefed on what he would say that afternoon. Political reporters from Britain's evening papers had to write their stories before Kinnock spoke if they were to meet their deadlines; morning briefings – in London as much as at Party conferences – are central to their work. That Tuesday morning they were shown what Kinnock would say about Liverpool's Militants and their practice of promising things that could not be delivered:

> I'll tell you what happens with impossible promises. You start with implausible resolutions, which are then pickled into a rigid dogma and you end with the grotesque chaos of a Labour council hiring taxis to scuttle around a city handing out redundancy notices to its own workers. I'm telling you, you can't play politics with people's jobs, with their homes, with their essential services.

The language was stark: the journalists knew they had a dramatic story. More than one had to be persuaded not to seek a reaction from Hatton ahead of the speech. When Kinnock spoke, he maintained the structure of that passage, but added a number of words, shown in italics below:

> I'll tell you what happens with impossible promises. You start with far-fetched resolutions. They are then pickled into a rigid dogma, *a code, and you go through the years sticking to that, out-dated, misplaced, irrelevant to the real needs*, and you end with grotesque chaos of a Labour council – *a LABOUR council* – hiring taxis to scuttle around a city handing out redundancy notices to its own workers. I'm telling you, *no matter how entertaining, how fulfilling to short-term egos – I'm telling you and you'll listen* – you can't play politics with people's jobs and with people's services or with their homes.

As written prose, the shorter version is undoubtedly better. But a speech is a creature of its occasion: its time, its audience and – in this instance – the reaction of those it lambasts. That afternoon Kinnock's task was not simply to denounce Militant, but to do as much as he could to destroy its appeal. The written speech contained the framework for denunciation; but as Kinnock approached that section – near the end of his speech – it was clear that much of the impact lay in the fine-tuning: his delivery, his final choice of words and the response of people around him.

As he began his assault, Hatton and his immediate allies were barely twenty feet away in the body of the hall. They were visibly angry. Some heckling began. This provoked counter-heckling by delegates hostile to Militant. At this point Kinnock could have kept his head down and stuck to his text. Instead he heightened the drama by adding words in a way that was bound to increase the reaction. By the time he had reached his comments about 'the grotesque chaos of a Labour council', Hatton was on his feet. Close-up television pictures showed Hatton shouting 'liar, liar'. This vivid confrontation was precisely what Kinnock sought. By repeating the phrase, and varying the emphasis – 'a Labour council – a LABOUR council' – Kinnock not only heightened the drama still further, but achieved the effect of releasing hundreds of other delegates from their anxieties about Liverpool and Militant. Their party leader was declaring war on the Trotskyists; most Labour delegates in the hall were relieved and delighted, and showed it.

More to the point, the television cameras showed their relief and their enthusiastic response to Kinnock's assault. This brief, telling episode was almost over, but not quite. As Kinnock completed his sentence about redundancy notices, Eric Heffer began to walk from the platform. Heffer was a Liverpool MP and a member of Labour's National Executive. He was not a Militant, but he was left-wing and had some sympathy with Liverpool's strategy of confrontation. He was appalled that a Labour Party leader should publicly attack a Labour council in this way.

Heffer's exit aroused more cheers and boos. Again, Kinnock had a choice about how to respond. Again, he added words – '. . . no matter how entertaining, how fulfilling to short-term egos . . .' – that seem unnecessary when seen in print some years later, but which carried an unmistakable message of determination amid the noise.

Finally, Kinnock brought this passage to a climax: 'I'm telling you – and you'll listen – you can't play politics with people's jobs and with

4

people's services or with their homes.' Although the operative words were much as in the written text, that sentence was lifted by Kinnock's response to the turmoil he had unleashed: 'I'm telling you – *and you'll listen* . . .' With that phrase, Kinnock asserted his authority in the manner of a victorious duellist raising his sword in triumph over a prostrate victim. He had won a decisive round in his battle against extremism. From the expression on his face as he issued his command – 'you'll listen' – he knew he had won; and so did almost everyone in the hall.

The impact of his speech was not confined to Bournemouth. A Harris poll conducted two days later for the *Observer* found that Kinnock had overtaken Margaret Thatcher for the first time as the person electors thought would 'make the best Prime Minister'. His rating had climbed fourteen points in just seven days.

*

This book contains the texts of eleven speeches Neil Kinnock has delivered to nine Party conferences since 1983. In 1983 and 1985 he spoke twice. In 1983 he spoke briefly on the evening of Sunday, 2 October, following the announcement of his election as leader; the following Thursday, he delivered a longer speech as leader-elect. (Michael Foot remained party leader until the end of the conference and therefore delivered the traditional Tuesday afternoon leader's speech.) In 1985, apart from his leader's speech in which he attacked Militant, Kinnock responded on the Wednesday morning to a debate on the miners' strike which had collapsed earlier that year. Those speeches, as well as his leader's speeches, are included here.

The speeches are printed as delivered, rather than as written. No circumlocutions have been excised or spare adjectives removed. The decision to present his speeches in this way was an easy one to take: to reprint simply the press handouts would be to give a slightly, but at times significantly, misleading impression of what Kinnock said. In 1991 he told the party conference that a Labour government would introduce fixed-term parliaments. Although he had made his views known in interviews, he had not incorporated them into a major speech before. He decided to include it in his 1991 speech following John Major's decision – leaked the previous evening – to postpone the general election until 1992. Kinnock's response came too late to be incorporated in the text printed on Tuesday morning and handed to journalists after lunch.

By their nature, transcripts of speeches serve accuracy more faithfully than they serve literature. Speeches, after all, are designed to be listened to rather than read. Words that look flat on the printed page sometimes come to life in the atmosphere of a conference hall. Sometimes: but not always. Any honest assessment of Kinnock's speeches must conclude that their quality varies – both within individual speeches and from year to year.

At his best, Kinnock is arguably the finest orator in modern British politics. As his attack on Militant in 1985 illustrated, there are times when he adds words to his prepared text deliberately and successfully. On those occasions he displays a skill that few other politicians can match. Yet those same words look long-winded when read in calm isolation instead of being heard in a hall erupting with noise.

Some devices invariably enchant the ear more than the eye. When Martin Luther King addressed the vast civil rights rally from the steps of the Lincoln Memorial in Washington in August 1963, he said 'I have a dream' eight times, and followed these almost immediately with nine injunctions to 'let freedom ring'. Carefully used, repetition can have a persuasive, almost hypnotic, impact; but it is a device that belongs to speeches, not essays.

Two of Kinnock's most effective speeches have employed repetition to great effect. At Bridgend, two days before the 1983 general election, he provided one of the few examples of powerful electioneering by anyone in that year's wretched Labour campaign:

If Margaret Thatcher is re-elected as Prime Minister on Thursday, *I warn you*.
I warn you that you will have pain – when healing and relief depend upon payment.
I warn you that you will have ignorance – when talents are untended and wits are wasted, when learning is a privilege and not a right.
I warn that you will have poverty – when pensions slip and benefits are whittled away by a Government that won't pay in an economy that can't pay.
I warn you that you will be cold – when fuel charges are used as a tax system that the rich don't notice and the poor can't afford. . . .

If Margaret Thatcher wins on Thursday – I warn you not to be ordinary; I warn you not to be young; I warn you not to fall ill; I warn you not to get old.

The following week, after Foot had announced his intention to resign as party leader and Kinnock quickly emerged as the likeliest candidate to succeed him, the *Economist* wanted to introduce its readers – especially its overseas readers – to him. The magazine reprinted parts of his Bridgend speech to demonstrate his powers of oratory.

Five years later, and far more daringly, he combined repetition with mockery to attack Thatcher's statement in a magazine interview that 'there is no such thing as society':

'No such thing as society', she says.
No obligation to the community.
No sense of solidarity.
No principles of sharing or caring.
'No such thing as society'.
No sisterhood, no brotherhood.
No neighbourhood.
No honouring other people's mothers and fathers.
No succouring other people's little children.
'No such thing as society'.
No number other than one.
No person other than me.
No time other than now.
No such thing as society, just 'me' and 'now'.
That is Margaret Thatcher's society.

That sequence, constructed almost as blank verse, was carefully written: it relied for its effect on precise rhythms. On other occasions, Kinnock has roused his audiences with feats of improvisation. One of these had a bizarre sequel: the death of Senator Joe Biden's ambitions in 1988 to win the Democratic nomination for the US presidency. He was caught cribbing Kinnock's speech to the annual conference of the Welsh Labour Party on 15 May 1987 – after Margaret Thatcher had announced the date of that year's election (11 June), but before the formal start of the campaign.

What is remarkable about Biden's plagiarism is not just that it occurred, but that an American politician employing full-time speech-writers raided a passage that appeared nowhere in the text Kinnock carried onto the platform. Its genesis was a series of notes jotted down in the back of a car on the way to the conference. When Kinnock rose to speak, he glanced at the notes and extemporized the words:

Why am I the first Kinnock in a thousand generations to be able to get to university? Was it because *all* our predecessors were 'thick'? Did they lack talent – those people who could sing, and play, and recite poetry; those people who could make wonderful, beautiful things with their hands; those people who could dream dreams, see visions; those people who had such a sense of perception as to know in times so brutal, so oppressive, that they could win their way out of that by coming together?

Were those people not university material? Couldn't they have knocked off their A-levels in an afternoon? But why didn't they get it? Was it because they were weak – those people who could work eight hours a day underground and then come up and play football? Weak? Those women who could survive eleven child-bearings, were they weak? Those people who could stand with their backs and legs straight and face the great – the people who had control over their lives, the ones that owned their workplaces and tried to own them – and tell them 'No, I won't take your orders.' Were they weak? Does anybody really think that they didn't get what we had because they didn't have the talent, or the strength, or the endurance, or the commitment? Of course not. It was because there was no platform on which they could stand.

As Kinnock spoke, one bulky Merseyside police officer – drafted into the town to help control the crowds – was seen with tears streaming down his face. In Llandudno Kinnock provided the first public sign that he would be a formidable campaigner during the 1987 election. (An extract from the speech was used in Hugh Hudson's celebrated Labour election broadcast the following Thursday.) Although Labour lost the election heavily, Kinnock's personal ratings rose sharply. At the start of the campaign only 18 per cent told Gallup that they regarded him as the most impressive campaigner among the four party leaders; by 9 June, two days before the election, that number had climbed to 43 per cent – more than the other three (Thatcher, David Steel and David Owen) combined.

Those figures, like the poll findings following the 1985 party conference, were exceptional – but only in the size of the shift in public opinion, not its direction. Each month MORI asks around 2,000 electors whether they are satisfied or dissatisfied with the performance of each of the main party leaders. Like other opposition leaders before him (notably Edward Heath in the late 1960s and Thatcher during the mid-1970s), Kinnock's ratings have usually lagged behind his rivals. But just as the 1987 election campaign lifted his ratings, so has every Labour Party conference since his election as leader:

KINNOCK'S RATINGS

Q. Are you satisfied or dissatisfied with the way Mr Kinnock is doing his job as leader of the Labour Party? (answers in percentages)

	September	October	Change
1984	29	30	+ 1
1985	30	43	+13
1986	32	40	+ 8
1987	36	38	+ 2
1988	32	36	+ 4
1989	39	43	+ 4
1990	41	45	+ 4
1991	33	41	+ 8

Source: MORI/*Sunday Times*

No other party leader has achieved that kind of record. When the evidence from the 1987 election is added, a clear message emerges: that when Kinnock enjoys sustained television exposure, and when voters are given the opportunity to judge him directly, he wins admirers. For more than eight years his set-piece speeches have provided a central element in that exposure. Views will differ about the quality of individual speeches; but as to their practical impact – the way voters receive them – there can be little doubt that most have been notable successes.

*

During the early years of Kinnock's leadership, much of his attention was directed at the dreadful state of the party he inherited. He took over in the wake of Labour's worst election result for two generations. Its support had dropped no fewer than ten points in four years to 28 per cent – only two points more than the Liberal/SDP Alliance.

The statistics told only part of the story. The election result saw the culmination of, and the price Labour paid for, two years of bitter division, a set of policies largely at odds with public sentiment, and a chaotically disorganised election campaign. Even these chronic failings did not embrace the whole of the crisis facing Labour in the autumn of 1983. When Kinnock became its leader, the party's long-term survival was in doubt, and its future ability to challenge seriously for power was widely derided.

In essence, the years leading up to that crisis had seen the collapse of an always precarious stand-off between the party's pragmatists and its radicals. The terms of that stand-off were never formally agreed, but almost everyone who mattered adhered to them as if bound by a solemn treaty. In opposition the pragmatists allowed the radicals to have their head; in government the radicals did not seriously try to stop the pragmatists running the country.

That arrangement was unsatisfactory in many ways, but it seemed to work; that is, Labour won as many elections as it lost. From time to time someone would challenge this state of affairs, but without success: Hugh Gaitskell failed in 1959/60 to persuade Labour to drop Clause IV, part IV of its constitution, which committed the party to social ownership; Tony Benn failed in the mid-1970s to persuade his cabinet colleagues to take industrial planning seriously.

After 1979, however, the radicals decided – not unreasonably from their point of view – that there was little point in devising far-reaching policies in opposition if the party leadership was going to ignore them in power. They correctly identified the party's constitution as the main stumbling block to socialism: from their point of view it gave too much power to Labour MPs and too little to party activists. The radicals made three demands: the party leader should be elected by the party as a whole, not just MPs; the procedures for deciding the content of election manifestos should be changed to make it harder to ignore policies agreed by the party's annual conference; and local constituency activists should have more powers to deselect Labour MPs and replace them with more congenial (i.e. more left-wing) candidates.

INTRODUCTION

By January 1981 the radicals had achieved two of their three aims: an electoral college had been established for electing the party's leader and deputy leader; and mandatory reselection contests had been introduced for MPs. The content of the party's election manifestos remained beyond the reach of the (then left-controlled) National Executive – although it seemed just a matter of time before the party leadership lost control of manifesto-drafting, too.

The immediate consequence of these constitutional upheavals was the defection of thirteen Labour MPs, including two former cabinet ministers, and the formation of the Social Democratic Party. By June 1982 they had been joined by another fourteen defectors. The defections helped to move Labour's own centre of gravity further to the left. When Tony Benn decided to use the new electoral college procedure to challenge Denis Healey for the post of deputy leader, he seemed to have a good chance of victory. In the event, Healey won – but by only 50.4 per cent of the vote to 49.6 per cent.

Kinnock – then Labour's education spokesman – played a decisive role in blocking Benn. As a member of the left-wing Tribune MP, he could not be expected to vote for Healey; yet he feared the prospect of a Benn victory – both for the party as a whole, and for the way it would undermine the authority of Michael Foot, Labour's leader and Kinnock's friend and mentor. Two weeks before the deputy leadership vote, Kinnock wrote a 3,000-word article for *Tribune*, saying that he would vote for fellow Tribune MP John Silkin in the first round of the contest but – following Silkin's inevitable elimination in the first round – would abstain in the second round. Kinnock based his decision on the grounds that Benn was a divisive candidate whose challenge had already harmed Labour and threatened to condemn the party to years in the political wilderness:

Those who scorn appeals for unity . . . desert the millions of people for whom a Labour Government would be the only means of deliverance from insecurity, poverty, unemployment and despair . . . I believe that Tony has fostered antagonism within the party, he has undermined the credibility of credible policies by oversimplification, he has not disowned those who insist upon support for his candidature as the test of loyalty to Labour policy. I believe that, through an inaccurate analysis of the position and power of the Labour movement and by a tactically mistaken

11

decision to contest the deputy leadership in 1981, Tony has significantly harmed the current standing and electoral opportunities of the Labour Party. By so doing he has inadvertently harmed those who I am sure he most wants to help.

— Tribune
23 September 1981

Kinnock's article was significant for three reasons. First, it demonstrated a degree of political courage. He put into words what many on the left thought but nobody of his stature had said; and he said it in the Left's own weekly newspaper. Second, the article worked. That is, thirty-seven Labour MPs abstained in the second round of the contest. Such was the closeness of the result that had just thirteen of those abstainers backed Benn, he would have won.

Third, Kinnock's article, and the abstentions, marked the beginning of a chain of events that was to lead eventually to the isolation, and finally impotence, of the radicals. Although Kinnock has changed his mind on a number of policies since the early 1980s – most obviously, on defence – he has for more than a decade used the same tools to remove the thorns of left-wing influence from the Labour Party. Starting with his *Tribune* article in September 1981, he has deployed a constant line of argument against the far Left: it lacks realism, it lacks commitment to party unity, and – above all – it lacks the will to win.

In retrospect, the odd thing is that any political leader should need to explain the virtues of realism, unity and victory. Yet such was the state of the Labour Party in the early 1980s that they were not self-evident; hence Kinnock's need to dwell on them in his conference speeches for most of the 1980s. Thus in 1983:

[The Conservatives] are the enemy: they must be defeated, and we must defeat them together. If we try by groups and factions, we will not do it. If we give greater attention to arguments between ourselves than to our enmity against them, we will not do it. If we give more attention to impressing each other than convincing the people we have to convince, we will not do it. They are the enemy. They must be defeated and we must defeat them together. That is our purpose. There must be no activity in this labour movement that is superior to that purpose.

Or 1984:

> Only one thing could possibly arrest [Labour's] recovery: amnesia,
> memory loss. It is an awful affliction for anyone. But for a political
> party it can be an absolutely crippling disease . . . And for this
> party, the vaccine is simply to recall what defeat felt like last year,
> and that should immunise each and every one of us completely
> against any attitude or activity that can impede our progress
> towards victory.

Or 1985:

> There are some in our movement who . . . accuse me of an
> obsession with electoral politics . . . I say to them . . . that there is
> an implacable need to win and there is an implacable need for us to
> understand that we address an electorate which is sceptical, an
> electorate which needs convincing . . .

Or 1987, after a further general election defeat.

> The price for division and disunity is paid most of all by those who
> attract our greatest concern, those who most need our help, those
> who most depend on our success. We cannot let them down, we
> must not let them pay that price again.

Those general statements provided the backdrop for a series of steps
that Kinnock took during his first eight years as leader to isolate the
far Left. Kinnock's method resembled that of a climber scaling an
awkward rock face: hammering pitons into tiny cracks, testing them
for strength, and making sure of each foothold before climbing
further. To any spectator hoping for a fast ascent, Kinnock's method
was slow and sometimes tedious. Yet at least he can claim to have
reached the summit. Previous leaders either failed to try or tried and
failed. At the margin, arguments remain about the speed and detailed
tactics of reform: could Kinnock have prepared better for the debate
in 1984 on one-member-one-vote in the selection of MPs, and avoided
an embarrassing defeat? Should he have been blunter in 1987 about
the need to jettison outdated practices? Yet after eight years, the
central point about Labour, as it prepares for the next general

election, is that it follows its leader more obediently than at any time for at least half a century.

*

Kinnock's speeches provide ample evidence of his piton-hammering technique. In 1984, after just one year as leader, he had to address a party conference that was largely preoccupied with the miners' strike that had begun six months earlier. Traditionally, few groups of workers could rely more confidently than the miners on the sympathy of ordinary Labour Party members. Yet their leader, Arthur Scargill, represented precisely the face of left-wing politics that Kinnock most despised: extreme, divisive and impossiblist. ('Impossiblist' is an ugly but useful word to describe the tactic of making demands that are bound to be rejected, in the hope that the process of struggle will win fresh converts for other battles later on. To Kinnock, Militant's stewardship of Liverpool City Council was largely an exercise in impossiblist politics; so was the miners' strike.)

Had the strike succeeded in forcing the Coal Board to abandon its plans to close pits, Kinnock's plans to reform the Labour Party would have been set back many years. There was, however, little danger of that. From its earliest week the strike was destined to fail. The issue quickly became one of blame. Would Scargill be shown up as a wild, inept leader – or Kinnock as a lukewarm ally, whose refusal to offer wholehearted support had amounted to betrayal?

There are two ways to view Kinnock's 1984 conference speech: as a cop-out, or as an act of ground-clearing for what he would say when the strike was over. He dealt with two issues: violence on the picket-lines, and the notion (favoured by some on the far Left) that the strike should be seen not just as an industrial dispute but as a legitimate act of political defiance against the government. On the first, Kinnock was extravagantly even-handed in his condemnation of 'all violence, without fear or favour'. On the second, he made the classic argument for respecting democracy and the rule of law:

> Democracy is the first premise of our socialism; it is a matter of principle, not of convenience; it is a matter of commonsense, not tactics . . .
>
> At the earliest possible time we want to pass and enforce laws to redress grievances; to promote justice and opportunity; to change

economic ownership and rewards. We want the power to do that –
so we cannot sharpen legality as our main weapon for the future,
and simultaneously scorn legality because it doesn't suit us at the
present time . . .

The people who need the support and safeguard of trade
unionism and of public services, cannot afford to be part of any
political 'Charge of the Light Brigade'. There is no glory in defeat
for them; there is nothing but extra miserable burdens of insecurity
and insufficiency. In those circumstances it is they – the poorest,
the weakest, and the most needy – who are the martyrs. That's the
fact.

What Kinnock did not do was address the wisdom of the strike or
the tactics of its leaders. His arguments in favour of legality were made
in terms of principle, not as a rebuke to the executive of the National
Union of Mineworkers. Not once here, or anywhere else in his speech,
did he refer directly to Scargill.

Had Kinnock done so, and attacked the miners' leader by name, he
would undoubtedly have won widespread praise. But he would also
have jeopardised the still fragile coalition he was trying to build within
the Labour Party, ranging from centre-left to centre-right, that he
needed in order to achieve his larger long-term ambitions. He was also
constrained by a particular kind of loyalty that outsiders often found
baffling. His own constituency contained many striking miners. As in
the rest of South Wales, they had struck out of solidarity rather than
conviction: the miners' leadership in Wales distrusted Scargill, but –
unlike the Nottinghamshire miners – remained loyal to the national
union. For Kinnock to have attacked the strike while it was still in
progress would have opened him to the charge of betraying the
principles of solidarity in general, and the striking miners back in
Islwyn in particular.

So Kinnock remained silent on the merits of the strike and bided his
time. He knew that he would face accusations of cowardice, but hoped
that time would vindicate his tactics. His chance to say what he really
felt would have to wait until the strike's inevitable defeat.

That opportunity came the following year. The strike collapsed in
March 1985. Scargill, however, attempted, in best impossiblist style,
to extract political capital from the defeat. His union tabled a motion
to the Labour conference calling on 'the next Labour government' to

reimburse the union with all the money that the courts had seized during the strike through fines and sequestration.

It is normal practice for party leaders to confine their conference speeches to the hour-long address that technically serves the function of a 'parliamentary report' to delegates. Other executive members are given the task of responding to particular debates and setting out the executive's view. The most widely remembered precedent for a party leader replying to a specific debate was not a happy one. In 1960 Hugh Gaitskell responded to the defence debate by declaring his opposition to unilateral nuclear disarmament and insisting that he would 'fight, fight and fight again to save the party we love'. He lost the vote and provoked the first ever challenge to a serving Labour Party leader.

In 1985 Kinnock decided to speak on behalf of the executive and oppose the miners' demands for reimbursement. His speech came on the morning following his set-piece attack on Militant. The difference was that Kinnock's speech on the miners was delivered from notes made during the debate, not read from a text written in advance. That means that the speech, reread some years later, has more rough edges than most. Yet its importance as a political document remains considerable, for the speech amounted to a sustained assault on the leadership of a major trade union.

Moreover, he levelled at Scargill a charge more damaging than that of extremism and more hurtful than that of disloyalty. He accused the miners' president of stupidity. Kinnock described the plight of miners who had incurred large debts during the strike, and continued:

> The question is asked, 'How did it come to that?' I will give you the answer of a lodge official in my constituency, a man who was on strike from the first day to the last, who picketed continuously, whose wife and family backed him to the hilt. He said to me . . . 'We knew there was a build-up of coal stocks . . . We knew that of all the times to call a coalmining strike, the end of the winter is just about the point in the calendar least appropriate . . .'
>
> The strike wore on, the violence built up because the single tactic chosen was that of mass picketing, and so we saw policing on a scale and with a system that has never been seen in Britain before. The court actions came, and by their attitude to the court actions, the NUM leadership ensured that they would face crippling

damages as a consequence. To the question, 'How did this position arise?', the man from the lodge in my constituency said, 'It arose because nobody really thought it out.'

It is a measure of his speech that Kinnock's bitter attack against Scargill received greater public notice than the result of the vote. By a narrow majority the conference backed the miners. But Kinnock had made it clear that he would have nothing to do with reimbursement if Labour came to power; and most of those who voted for Scargill's motion knew they had won an empty victory.

After 1985 Scargill's influence in the trade union movement waned, as pits continued to close and his union shrank. Kinnock had waited to assert his politics over those of the NUM leadership until he judged the time was right, and his piton would hold. It did. In the space of twenty-four hours Kinnock had condemned both of the causes that the far Left had hoped would revive their fortunes – reimbursement for the miners, and militancy in local government. As a result of his speeches, and their evident popularity with the wider public, the centre-left-to-centre-right coalition grew in strength – in the unions, among Labour MPs and within the national executive. However, the struggle to modernise Labour's policies had only just begun.

*

Labour Party programme in 1992 bears little similarity to the manifesto on which it lost the 1983 general election. Among the policies that have been abandoned are: withdrawal from the European Community; unilateral nuclear disarmament; import controls; price controls; complete repeal of the Conservatives' trade union laws; and the establishment of 'a significant public stake in electronics, pharmaceuticals, health equipment and building materials'.

Different policies have changed at different times. Even before he became party leader, Kinnock had announced his acceptance of British membership of the European Community. On this, as on some other occasions, he made his announcement not to the annual party conference but to a more directly affected audience: in September 1983 he visited the European Parliament at Strasbourg and told Labour's eighteen members – most of whom had long supported a policy of withdrawal – that under his leadership the party would take a more positive view of Community membership.

On trade union policies, likewise, Kinnock saved his main speeches for union audiences. In September 1988 he spoke at the annual meeting of the Trades Union Congress and urged unions to take part in the Government's new Employment Training programme – even though many unionists were advocating a boycott. Two years later he returned to the TUC and argued that unions should not expect a special, cosy relationship with a future Labour government.

His 1990 speech to the TUC followed his appointment of Tony Blair ten months earlier as Shadow Employment Secretary. Blair wanted to change some of the policies he had inherited from Michael Meacher, his predecessor. As a barrister who had specialised in labour law before becoming an MP, Blair brought a blend of flexibility and expertise to the post. He wanted to modify rather than undo the Conservatives' union laws; this meant that the unions would have to accept a continuation of the use of ballots, limits to strike action, a clear legal framework for industrial relations disputes, and an end to closed shops. Not surprisingly, Blair's reforms were keenly debated at the TUC in September 1990. Opposition to Blair's policies was led by Arthur Scargill. He accused the party leadership of a 'betrayal of principle', and argued that unions were entitled to 'special favours' from a Labour government. Scargill's view was heavily defeated; but his speech opened Kinnock's way to an assault as vehement as anything the party leader had said in 1984 or 1985. Referring to Scargill's comments about 'betrayal of principle', Kinnock said:

That's a serious charge to make – and it's absolutely wrong. Principles are basic values that must guide at all times. But unless they can be turned into action, unless they can be put into power and applied in practice, they really are of very little comfort to the needy, they right very few wrongs.

That might not impress those who think that principles are best cherished in opposition. They might be comfortable listening to the sound of their own self-righteousness. But I must say that it's not those people who suffer for the lack of power. And I have to tell you that I think it's a pretty strange set of principles that produces martyrdom for the followers and never sacrifice for the leaders.

Yesterday, I heard a voice here also saying that what was needed was 'special favours'. I have to tell him that the purpose of what we do is not 'favours' – it's justice, it's rights. Of course, we're all friends, aren't we? We'll do what we can to help each other along the way, won't we? But you can't depend on favours to gain progress for a society.

Decent pensions aren't a favour – they are justice. Decent health treatment in a free health service isn't a favour – it's justice. Good housing, good education, isn't a favour – it's justice. Equal opportunities for women and men aren't favours, they are justice. The right to join a trade union, the right to vote, the right to be recognised upheld in law aren't favours – they are justice. When we restore entitlements of trade union membership to GCHQ workers it won't be as a favour but as a civil right.

Surely it's basic to us that these must be rights of citizenship, not gifts of patronage, not favours. As a democratic socialist and a trade unionist I say – leave the favouritism, leave the back-handers, leave the nepotism, leave the insider-dealing and the old boy system to the Tories and their 'friends of the family'. That is their way.

Our way is different. It is the way of equality, or merit, of civil rights, of justice without fear and without favour. That is what this movement was created to gain. It wasn't born in favours, it wasn't built on favours, it doesn't live by favours and won't have a future by favours.

*

Kinnock's party conference speeches, then, do not provide a complete trace of his changes of policy. But in two of the most sensitive subjects, they do illuminate important parts of his trajectory. The more complex and fundamental of the two concerns Kinnock's views about the function of the state and the role of the markets.

Before 1987, every reference Kinnock made to market forces was critical. He did not propose the creation of a command economy – but neither did he say what good, if any, market forces ever did. Thus, in 1984 he said:

That is why we are socialists; that is why we seek power – to seek mastery of change for the benefit of the people. If we don't, we shall see with terrible speed, and with awful results, the irrational response to technological and economic change which the market economy and the social market economy makes, and has always made – huge numbers of unemployed, millions more who live in constant fear of unemployment and the insecurity which it brings . . .

And in 1986:

> None of the major social, commercial, industrial or employment problems that we face is self-correcting. The market will not look after those problems; it can only worsen those problems. If they are to be overcome, systematic planned action must be taken by government, and it must be taken in concert with all the participants in the economy, to construct the framework of the educational, scientific, technical and social conditions within which this country can thrive again.

The significance of those remarks lies in their tone more than the detailed policies they implied. The idea of intervening in market forces to produce broad economic, industrial and social objectives is not itself left-wing: Michael Heseltine devoted part of his efforts as a Conservative backbench MP between 1986 and 1990 to opposing laisser-faire economics and arguing for an active industrial policy by the government. What gave Kinnock's remarks their tone of hostility to market forces was their absence of any recognition that markets, properly harnessed, do promote prosperity.

West Germany's Social Democratic Party (SPD) had acknowledged this very point almost three decades earlier. In 1959, at a conference in Bad Godesberg – held after three successive defeats in Federal elections – the SPD explicitly rejected a political strategy based on comprehensive public ownership. In its new programme the SPD declared:

> Free choice of consumer goods and services, free choice of working place, freedom for employers to exercise their initiative as well as free competition are essential conditions of a Social democratic economic policy . . . Private ownership of the means of production can claim protection by society as long as is does not hinder the establishment of social justice.

The ideological thrust of the SPD's Bad Godesberg programme was summed up by the formula: 'As much competition as possible: as much planning as necessary'. Kinnock's speeches before 1987 invoked the second half of that formula, but were silent on the first half.

After 1987, however, Kinnock's position changed. Like the SPD in 1959, Labour had now lost three successive elections; and like the SPD, it badly needed to find a more appealing ideology. In his speech to Labour's conference four months after that defeat. Kinnock started the process that was to end in Labour's comprehensive embrace of the virtues of competition:

> Ours is a socialism . . . that knows that whilst the market is an adequate system for deciding the price and availability of many goods and services, the market has not been, is not, and never will be an adequate mechanism for deciding upon the supply or quality of health care and education and so much else that is fundamental to a decent life. The market alone will never be adequate for determining the quantity of investment in science or in the arts. And the market alone will never ensure that flow of investment in machines, people, skills and ideas which is necessary to gain and sustain long-term economic strength and the employment that comes with it.

The thrust of Kinnock's remarks remained critical of the market but for the first time he acknowledged its uses as 'an adequate system for deciding the price and availability of many goods and services'. Moreover, his subsequent criticisms were not of 'the market' but of 'the market alone'. The addition of 'alone' was significant. Consider these two statements: 'I shall not visit my in-laws'; and: 'I shall not visit my in-laws alone'. Both announcements imply wariness, but they signal different practical consequences.

Kinnock's 1988 speech bent the direction of party policy still further:

> There are those, like the government, who simply say 'private good, public bad'. There are those who say, in a mirror image, 'public good, private bad'. Neither of them are dealing with the realities . . . Neither are asking the real question 'does it work?' But that test is applied elsewhere. It is applied in Germany, in

Japan, in Sweden, in France. In all of those countries they appreciated long ago that public and private sectors, government and market, had to work *in combination* if the strength of the economy was to be developed and the potential of the economy to be maximised . . .

Comrades, the day may come when this conference, this movement, is faced with a choice of socialist economies. The debate will be fascinating as the Labour Party conference chooses between the two. But until that day comes . . . the fact is that the kind of economy we will be faced with when we win the election will be a market economy. That is what we have to deal with and we will have to make it work better than the Tories do.

There, for the first time, Kinnock positively delighted in the power of market forces. His plea for even-handedness had clear echoes of the Bad Godesberg programme. The detailed implications of this ideological shift subsequently became apparent with the publication of Labour's policy review documents, *Meet the Challenge, Make the Change* (1989), *Looking to the Future* (1990) and *Opportunity Britain* (1991). By 1991, Labour had abandoned all thoughts of price control for private industry, and almost all thoughts of returning privatised companies to public ownership.

In his 1991 conference speech, Kinnock returned to the subject of markets. The party's transformation was now complete. Competition was good, while the role of the Government was not so much to take 'systematic planned action' as to 'share a sense of responsibility' with the private sector:

[Other EC] governments, socialist, conservative, coalition governments – whatever else separates them – share a sense of responsibility. They know that it is a prime duty of modern democratic government to create the conditions for business to succeed and for individuals and communities to thrive . . .

We will help to create a modern industrial economy to compete and succeed in the Single Market . . . An innovation-driven economy needs a tax system and economic policies which promote sustained investment. It needs monopolies and mergers regulations that promote competition and safeguard company programmes of research and development. We shall make those changes.

22

With those words, Kinnock signalled his embrace of a central feature of the revisionists' creed: that the state should no longer aspire to be a major player in industry, but instead adopt the role of umpire and rule-maker. The collapse of communism in eastern Europe had undoubtedly eased his way in coaxing Labour down the revisionist path: he no longer had to waste energy arguing against those left-wingers who used to argue with a straight face that working people enjoyed a higher quality of life in the communist east than the capitalist west. But the fact remained that Kinnock had transformed Labour's ideological ambitions; and in this he had succeeded where Gaitskell, in particular, had failed.

*

Changing Labour's defence policy was in some ways easier and in some ways harder than changing its attitude to market forces. It was easier in the sense that the central issue was unconnected with ideology: should Britain abandon nuclear weapons regardless of the actions of other countries, or should disarmament be a matter of circumstance and negotiation? Although some advocates of uni-lateralism maintained that their stand was rooted in socialism, a glance at other countries rather undermined this attitude. Thus socialist France still maintained the *force de frappe*, while Ireland, steeped in reactionary social values and dominated by two right-wing parties, countenanced no nuclear installations of any kind on its soil.

However, the very stark nature of the issue also made a change of policy harder to achieve. Kinnock was able to craft his new policy towards markets in stages, but he could not perform the same trick with defence. There was no middle way between unilateralism and multilateralism: abandonment of nuclear weapons was either party policy or it was not. It followed that if Labour was to switch from unilateralism to multilateralism, the moment of that switch would inevitably be one of public drama.

Defence presented Kinnock with a further, more personal difficulty. His rise within the party had been that of a left-winger who had publicly identified himself with the Campaign for Nuclear Disarmament. In his 1981 *Tribune* article where he explained why he could not vote for Tony Benn, he also set out his reasons for not supporting Denis Healey. The most prominent reason was Healey's multilateralism.

Kinnock was, of course, associated with other policies before 1983 that he subsequently changed; but for many Labour Party members, none had a resonance to compare with their feelings towards nuclear weapons. At root the issue was apparently simple and about moral principle. Its simplicity made the argument more accessible than say, debates about the future of the Common Agricultural Policy or the organisation of the steel industry. The use of moral principle roused passions, but at the same time inhibited open debate: if it was wrong to own nuclear weapons, then it was wrong in all circumstances and at all times. Even to ask the question, 'should we re-examine our unilateralism?' was to invite accusations of compromise and even treachery.

As with Kinnock's references to the role of markets, his remarks about defence fall clearly into pre-1987 and post-1987 sections. In his 1984 conference speech, for example, Kinnock presented the normal, straightforward argument for unilateralism:

> We need the power to provide the effective defence of our country, and our values, by meeting the obligations of modern conventional defence and of alliance – without nuclear weapons, which by their possession make us a nuclear target and would by their use terminate our existence and all future forms of existence.

In 1985 Kinnock enlisted a speech made three months earlier to the House of Lords by Field Marshal Lord Carver. Carver was a former Chief of the Defence Staff; he said the first priority of Britain's defence policy should be 'our conventional forces . . . not illusions of nuclear grandeur'. Kinnock endorsed Carver's speech, saying that it demonstrated

> the insanity, the waste, the illusion of Tory Party policy, and . . . the reality and necessity of our complete non-nuclear defence policy to maintain the proper security of our country and alliance. That is our policy, our commitment to the British people, and we will honour it in full.

In 1986 Kinnock made the same point in more vivid and personal terms:

I tell you in no casual spirit, no bravado, that like most of my fellow citizens I would if necessary fight and die, fight and lay down my life for my country, but I tell you I would never let my country die for me.

However, in the same speech, Kinnock also went further than he had before to affirm his loyalty to the NATO alliance:

I hold it to be self-evident that it is the first duty of any government to ensure the security of the country over which it governs . . . Meeting that obligation requires that we defend ourselves effectively by land, sea and air and that we participate properly in the Alliance of which we are full and firm members.

Kinnock's Conservative opponents argued that his policy was hopelessly contradictory: how could Britain remain a 'full and firm' member of the Alliance if it repudiated a central feature of NATO strategy? The same point was made from the other end of the spectrum – by a minority of Labour Party members who favoured withdrawal from NATO.

In the 1987 general election, opinion polls showed that Labour's defence policy had cost the party votes. The conclusion drawn by Kinnock's closest advisers was not that the haemorrhage had made the difference between victory and defeat, but that it had turned a modest defeat into a rout.

Between 1987 and 1989 a new defence policy was designed as part of Labour's policy review. In his 1987 conference speech, Kinnock skirted the issue, saying nothing about British nuclear weapons and confining himself to complementary remarks about the Soviet–American talks on intermediate nuclear force reductions. In 1988, however, following a summer of confusion for which Kinnock himself was largely to blame (see page 144 below), he decided to pave the ground in his conference speech for a switch to multilateralism:

This party, I am certain, wants to be part of the process of nuclear disarmament. Indeed, this party wants to take a leading part in that process of nuclear disarmament. That is only possible in government. It is not possible out of government. When we conclude our review next year and when we resolve our policy for fighting the next general election, that policy must be serious about nuclear disarmament, serious about defence. Indeed, so serious about both objectives that we are capable of earning the democratic power to achieve them.

The key word in that passage, twice repeated, is 'serious'. Kinnock's clear, but still unspoken, implication was that those who hankered after unilateralism were not serious about power: they would rather remain pure and in opposition than adjust to the mood of an electorate that rejected unilateralism.

By the following spring, the policy review was completed, and the explicit switch made to multilateralism. Labour's new policy was drafted by Gerald Kaufman and Martin O'Neill, the party's shadow foreign and defence secretaries, and published in *Meet the Challenge, Make the Change*. It promised that an incoming Labour government would: 'adopt a policy of no first use of Britain's nuclear capability'; 'seek to place all of Britain's nuclear capability . . . into international nuclear disarmament negotiations'; and 'immediately end testing of all British nuclear divices'. But Labour would not rid Britain of its nuclear weapons other than as a result of international disarmament negotiations.

In April 1989, at a two-day meeting of Labour's executive called to discuss *Meet the Challenge, Make the Change*, Kinnock spelt out his conversion to multilateralism. (Although the meeting was private, Peter Mandelson, Labour's director of communications, subsequently issued the text of Kinnock's remarks.)

Many in this room have protested and marched in support of nuclear disarmament. I have done something else: I have gone to the White House, the Kremlin, the Elysée, and argued the line for unilateral nuclear disarmament. I knew they would disagree with the policy. But above that, they were totally uncomprehending that we should want to get rid of nuclear missile systems without getting the elimination of nuclear weapons on other sides too – without getting anything for it in return. I argued for the policy because of the integrity of the objective of eliminating nuclear weapons. But I am not going to make that tactical argument for the unilateral abandonment of nuclear weapons without getting anything in return. I will not do it. The majority of the party and the majority of the country don't expect me to.

INTRODUCTION

Two fundamental questions remained. First, if Kinnock now intended that a Labour government should keep nuclear weapons, at least for the time being, would he be prepared to use them? In the past – most notably in his 1986 conference speech – he had vowed never to do so. A few days after the executive had backed the shift to multilateralism, Kinnock addressed the question of whether he would press the button. His audience – as for his 'thousand generations' speech at the start of the 1987 election campaign – was the Welsh Labour Party conference:

> We will negotiate with Trident and with the policy line that comes with all that operational weaponry, the policy line that never says 'yes' or 'no' to the question, 'will you press the nuclear button?' That is the combination of nuclear weaponry and the doctrine of uncertainty that is woven into it that we shall inherit. And it is that combination, the whole package, that we shall use in negotiations to secure nuclear disarmament by ourselves and by others. It is an inextricable combination, and the reason for that is that as long as the weapons exist, the assumption by others will be that there may be circumstances in which those weapons might be used.

Thus Kinnock did not completely overturn his previous declarations about the use of nuclear weapons. By relying on the doctrine of uncertainty, he located the power of deterrence in the *fact* of ownership and the *possibility* of use.

The second question was not finally answered until 1991: would a Labour government be willing to give up *all* of Britain's nuclear weapons in exchange for *some* reciprocal disarmament by Russia – and thus leave Britain at some future point without adequate means of deterring some future nuclear threat? Eventually Kaufman wrote an article for the *Guardian*, stating that Labour would keep some nuclear weapons as long as any potential aggressor possessed any.

In October 1989, six months after the new policy was unveiled, Kinnock defended it before the party conference. This could have been an awkward occasion – and had Kinnock attempted to abandon unilateralism any earlier, might well have resulted in humiliation. But not only had opinion inside the party now shifted (a pro-unilateralist resolution was defeated at the 1989 conference by a margin of three-to-two), the end of the Cold War was in sight. Kinnock could present his U-turn as a new policy for a new, exhilarating but still dangerous age:

> In the still deep divisions of ideology between East and West there are of course suspicions and rivalries built up over more than seventy years, which are not going to vanish in a year, or in five years or maybe even in ten years. Because of that, security will continue to mean armed security. But it must also increasingly mean – and does increasingly mean – the security of negotiated disarmament and the security of developing social and economic relationships . . . A new dual-track towards security is being built, not a bit like the old one. On it, the efforts for negotiated disarmament are running alongside increasing economic engagement.

By 1991, unilateralism was no longer a live issue within the Labour Party. It belonged to a buried, if not forgotten, past. Kinnock had no need to justify the continued possession of the bomb; he could concentrate instead on selling his policy's positive virtues:

> [The world] changed for the better again last Friday when President Bush announced his fresh initiative for disarmament on an unprecedented scale. Britain must be part of that progress. We must be part of the new negotiations on verifiable disarmament. And we should be doing everything possible to bring in the other nuclear powers, to halt and reverse proliferation, and to secure agreements to end testing of nuclear devices.

Eight years earlier, Kinnock had become party leader promising a defence policy that threatened upheavals within NATO. Now he presented himself as an apostle of continuity. And he had caused his party to traverse its U-turn without imploding into civil war. Of all his accomplishments within the party, this was the one that some most wanted, others most feared – and fewest thought possible with so little blood on the floor.

*

After eight years as leader, Kinnock has cast off the main policy albatrosses that had hung round Labour's neck in the early eighties.

28

He has secured large changes to the party's approach to defence, Europe, nationalisation, taxation, trade unions and the role of the state. He has also embarked on a programme to modernise the party's constitution, to make it more democratic. Important work remains to be done: on defining the party's view on electoral reform, for example, and completing the party's transition to one-member-one-vote democracy. Yet to a large extent Kinnock has stamped his authority on the party to a degree that Gaitskell, Wilson, Callaghan and Foot would have envied – and to a degree that Kinnock himself was unable to achieve prior to 1987.

The congruence between Labour's policies and Kinnock's own desires has a particular lesson for the coming election. In the past Kinnock has been at his best when he has shaken off his inhibitions and stated publicly what he has believed privately: as in his assault on Militant in 1985, or his 'fairness, not favours' speech to the TUC in 1990. He has been at his most long-winded and least persuasive when he has attempted to justify policies which he has been itching to alter. Many examples can be found in interviews in the mid-1980s on defence, taxation and nationalisation.

As Labour has changed, his discomfort has diminished. It is no accident that, by general agreement, he made one of his most effective Commons speeches in December 1991 on a pair of subjects where he used to be mocked: the European Community and policy towards sterling. In the debate on the results of the Maastricht summit of EC leaders, Kinnock was confident of his material and his arguments. Far from being derailed by Conservative interruptions, as he had been so often in the past, he relished them.

In interviews, too, his command of the detail of Labour's policies has begun to be noticed. In January 1992 he was interviewed at length by three senior *Financial Times* journalists. They observed in their report the following day:

> When we went to interview him in his office at the House of Commons yesterday we found him in good humour, confident, in control of his responses. His many detractors will regard this as a revelation . . . He gave full answers, but he did not ramble. He avoided more than a modicum of sub-clauses and dialectical by-ways. His language was in better focus than on many past occasions, private or public. He is still quite capable of living down

to his poor image. But equally, if he performs on TV as he has demonstrated he can do in small gatherings – and sporadically in the Commons – he will be no easy mark for the Conservatives. To the extent that they are banking on the windbag image to see them through the campaign they may be in for a surprise.

—Financial Times
23 January 1992

If Labour wins the coming election, its victory will be unusually sweet for its leader. Kinnock has spent eight years plucking thorns from his side, not all of them placed there by the Conservatives or unfriendly newspapers. Triumph at the polls would vindicate his strategy since 1983 and, for the time being at least, provide a conclusive response to his detractors.

The corollary, however, is that defeat would also be laid at Kinnock's door. Kinnock could blame Labour's defeats in 1983 and 1987 on outdated policies, poor discipline, and recent memories of extremist influence. Now, in 1992, those alibis have gone. Moreover, Labour is preparing to fight the election against a background of recession and rising unemployment.

The obvious conclusion is that Neil Kinnock has so completely fashioned Labour to his own design, that if it loses again, he will have no alibis left and ought to resign. That would undoubtedly be the case were he to have imposed his strategy on an unwilling party that wanted to resist his changes but feared to complain. In fact, the essence of Kinnock's style has been to construct robust coalitions through persuasion, rather than suppress debate by demanding loyalty. That is why the process of modernising Labour has taken so long. He could have run a command party and done many things faster. But the leaders of command parties, like the rulers of command economies, have a fragile power base, prone to collapse when things go wrong. Within the Conservative Party, both Edward Heath and Margaret Thatcher were removed, in effect by internal party coups.

One result of Kinnock's slower, surer method of leading his party is that his position is more secure. All of Labour's most prominent politicians – and certainly anyone who might succeed Kinnock in the near future – share both credit and responsibility for the party's electoral appeal.

INTRODUCTION

Whether Labour wins or loses, therefore, Kinnock will be hard to dislodge. He is far more likely to choose the time of his departure than be forced to resign against his will. For the main lesson of the past eight years is clear: Labour has not been transformed by Kinnock alone – but without Kinnock, Labour could not have been transformed at all.

Peter Kellner
February 1992

1983
BRIGHTON

'We must defeat them together'

Kinnock delivered two speeches at Labour's conference in 1983 – a short reply on the evening of Sunday 2 October to the announcement of his election as party leader; and a longer address on Thursday afternoon, 6 October.

His election had come as no surprise. For some weeks it had been clear that he had the backing of most trade unions and local constituency parties. Nevertheless, the scale of his victory was greater than most people expected. He won 92 per cent of the votes cast by local parties (which wielded 30 per cent of the votes in Labour's new 'electoral college' system for electing its leader and deputy leader) and 73 per cent of the votes of affiliated organisations – overwhelmingly trade unions (40 per cent of the college).

Kinnock fell just short of winning an overall majority among Labour MPs (who wielded the remaining 30 per cent); but he still enjoyed almost twice as much support as his main rival, Roy Hattersley. Altogether, Kinnock won 71.3 per cent of the electoral college vote, while Hattersley won 19.3, Eric Heffer 6.3 and Peter Shore 3.1.

The far Left knew that it could do nothing to prevent Kinnock's overwhelming victory. It did, however mount a strong challenge against Hattersley for the deputy leadership. In particular, it hoped that Michael Meacher would win more support than Hattersley among local constituency parties, which had traditionally voted for left-wing candidates in National Executive elections. However, at least 200 local parties decided their vote by one-member-one-vote ballots – and these opted for Hattersley by more than two-to-one. Their votes, combined with Hattersley's strong lead among trade unions and MPs, allowed him to win 67.3 per cent of the electoral college overall, to Meacher's 27.9 per cent. Meacher commanded majority support among those constituencies that had confined their decision to their general committee activists – but lagged well behind Hattersley in all other sections of the electoral college. The deputy leadership ballot provided clear evidence that any large-scale shift to one-member-one-vote ballots would erode the far Left's power – both in National Executive elections, and in the selection of parliamentary candidates.

Kinnock began his acceptance speech by echoing a comment he had made following a car accident some weeks earlier on the M4. His car had careered off the road; he was lucky to emerge unscathed. At the time he said: 'Someone up there must like me.' (At the time of his accident Kinnock had been playing a cassette of Brahms's Symphony No. 1; this music was subsequently used widely in Labour's 1987 general election campaign.)

*

During his longer main speech four days later, Kinnock invoked not only Michael Foot and Aneurin Bevan, but also Jack Jones, who had retired in 1978 as general secretary of the transport workers' union. Jones had been wounded in 1938 in the Spanish civil war, where he had fought for the international brigade; following his retirement he had launched a campaign to fight for pensioners' rights, and remained a familiar figure at labour Party conferences.

PK

ACCEPTANCE SPEECH

ON BEHALF of myself and the new deputy leader I should like to thank this conference. This movement has done us both a great honour and has offered us a great duty. We shall repay the honour and we shall serve the duty by leading this movement to victory in the next general election. That is what we are going to do. I should like for reasons that I think everyone will understand, to congratulate the Labour movement for its special audacity in electing me, when all of our earnest and generous friends and counsellors in the press, with the greatest desire to help the Labour Party as usual, were counselling strongly against it. All I can say is that, in the teeth of some of the advice, someone down here must like me too. Thank you very much.

There are clearly many in the movement whom I would want to thank, in the constituencies and the trade unions, in the affiliated organisations. Most particularly in my own constituency of Islwyn, my constituents without whose assistance I could not be here, and my marvellous colleagues and friends in the Islwyn Constituency Labour Party. I want to thank the campaign team and, indeed, everybody else's campaign team in this election, because what we proved in this election is that we can have democracy without enmity, that we can have contest without conflict, and that has done us good and has built our strength.

Those campaign teams must now weld together and get much bigger. Indeed they must embrace the whole Labour movement from this day on, right through the next victory. That is the Labour movement – one great campaign team, campaigning with each other, for each other, but, most of all, for the emancipation of the British people, the release of the yoke of Thatcherism, the reintroduction of prosperity into our country, to produce our way to prosperity, to get rid of the menace, the dangers, the vast costs of rearmament in our time.

There are just two other people that I want to thank. The first is the present leader of the Labour Party. I shall have much more to say about that on other occasions, but now I want to take this opportunity when we are all gathered together – I suspect there may be one or two colleagues looking into their televisions as well – to say that we thank Michael Foot for his special strengths of decency and courage in the face of the unmitigated adversity of the last three years. I want to thank him, too, for a past, present and future in which he has, he is and he will be an inspiration, a glowing inspiration to all of us who believe that the purpose of socialism is the gaining of liberty for humankind. We owe it to Michael Foot to advance that cause.

Finally I want to thank Glenys and my family. They tolerate me out of love, they raise my spirits. And I will tell you something else: I look at the future of their generation, and it makes me determined that they must not know war. It makes me determined that they shall not live in a world of want. I look at those children of mine, and at other people's children, and I say that the new generation shall not inherit idleness, ugliness or the prejudices of racism and sexism. I want those freedoms for my children, and I know that I cannot offer them to my children unless we are about the business of securing for all children of all people those same freedoms.

Here in this crowded, dangerous, beautiful world, there is only hope if there is hope *together* for all peoples. Our function, our mission, our objective as socialists is to see that we gain the power to achieve that. And there is no other way to achieve it but by socialism, by the deliberate organisation of all the resources of humankind, all of the talents of humankind. That is the definition of socialism – productive, systematic, liberating socialism. Socialism that does not count its greatness in the number of warheads that it has. Socialism that is determined to see that our country produces its way out of slump. Socialism that will take real pride and enjoy real patriotism when the sick, the old and the young and the poor have their just share of the wealth of this massively prosperous country.

To get that we have to win, and we must be of the people, and for the people. If we want guidance in how to win, we look no further than the man you would expect me to quote on this day of all days, Aneurin Bevan, my fellow countryman, my fellow townsman, my inspiration. Nye said, as a maxim for a political leader, and I commend it as a maxim for a political movement.

He who would lead must articulate the wants, the frustrations and the aspirations of the majority. Their hearts must be moved by his word, and so his words must be attuned to their realities. If he speaks in the old false categories, they will listen and at first nod their heads, for they hear a familiar echo from the past; but if he persists, they begin to appreciate that he is no longer with them. He must speak with the authentic accents of those who elected him. That means that he should share their values, that is be in touch with their realities.

That is not just my maxim, or Roy's maxim, or the maxim of any member of a shadow cabinet or National Executive Committee or a trade union leader or Member of Parliament. It is the maxim of the whole of this movement. We have to commend the commonsense of socialism, the realism of socialism, for that is how we get the maxim of socialism – the most rational, reasonable, emancipating creed ever put on to the agenda of humankind for the advancement of humankind. That is how we win. If anyone wants to know why we must conduct ourselves in this fashion, just remember at all times, with all temptations, how you, each and every one of you sitting in this hall, each and every Labour worker watching this conference, each and every Labour voter, yes, and some others as well, remember how you felt on that dreadful morning of 10 June. Just remember how you felt then, and think to yourselves: 'June the Ninth, 1983; never ever again will we experience that'.

Show that we understand it; show that we mean it; show that we know, taught by the hardest school of events, that unity is the price of victory. Not unity four weeks before the next general election, not unity before the European assembly elections, not unity before the local elections next year – but unity here and now and from henceforth. Not a cosmetic disguise, but living, working unity of people, of a movement, of a party, of a belief, of a conviction that wants to win. We want to win to save our country, to save our world. That is the fight.

We can enjoy fraternity between socialists and we must enjoy fidelity to socialism. If we put both, press both, explain both, teach both, listen about both, attune ourselves to the realities of the people whom we must impress – as Bevan recommends, it is not just that we can win, we *will* win.

LEADER-ELECT'S SPEECH

ON SUNDAY of this week I thanked you for electing me leader of the Labour Party. I thank you again, not just for electing me, but for giving me such immense support. In its breadth and depth, it offered me a duty and it gave me an authority to insist that the single purpose of my leadership will be to advance the cause of Labour and to secure victory of this party.

That must be the single cause, not just of leadership but of membership too. I want to thank you for accepting that obligation and demonstrating this week that you do accept that obligation of securing victory for the Labour Party: to thank you for the way in which you all have approached the Labour Party conference this week, the way in which in every contribution, in every action you have demonstrated your understanding of what we must do as a party.

The letters and the calls coming in from all over this country, as you know when you call home yourself, are saying in hundreds of messages, thousands of messages indeed, 'we are glad to be Labour; we are proud to be Labour'. The people are writing in who have been watching and listening to this conference and saying that they are thrilled by the conduct and the content of the Labour Party conference this week. That is how we are going to win. They are the people that we have to impress, the people that we have to convince, the people that we have to encourage, and we have begun to do it. We will continue to do it.

On Sunday night I thanked Michael Foot too; typically, he almost immediately responded with a magnificent speech on Tuesday that inspired the whole conference. On that occasion, and given my election to the leadership, I recalled another of many speeches that I have heard Michael make. On the particular occasion I have in mind it was a much shorter speech, no Beethovens about it, not even a chord from Brahms. On that occasion it was the first speech that he made as leader to the Parliamentary Labour Party. He quoted Aneurin Bevan – the last conversation that he had with him. Aneurin Bevan said to Michael Foot on his deathbed: 'Never underestimate the passion for unity, and do not forget it is the decent instinct of people who want to do something.' Over these past years Michael Foot has been driven entirely by that passion for unity because he is the most decent of men and because he wanted to do something, indeed everything, to advance our party and save our country.

Those instincts, those passions, that decency, must drive all of us now to the same degree. This week has been one of soaring encouragement, both for us here and for those in this country who have voted Labour, who want to vote Labour and, indeed, even for some who have never voted Labour before. For they see in us the only dependable means of defence against the current government, the only dependable means of advance to a different level of civilisation in our country. They want us and we reach out to them, but no one will consider this week to be anything more than a beginning. We have much to do. We have to win elections at every level; we have to recruit; we have to win over 100 seats in order to give us a parliamentary majority.

It would be a terrible mistake to underestimate the task, but it would be an almost equal mistake to overestimate the task. I say to you, comrades, without a shred of complacency, I ask you: despite our dreadful defeat on June 9, do we begin where the socialists of Greece and Spain and Portugal had to begin just a few years ago, coming out of exile, coming out of prison? We do not begin there with all those disadvantages.

Do we begin, as they had to, without even a rudimentary framework of democracy to give them the strength, the means, to make an approach to the people? Do we begin, as the French Socialist Party did ten years ago, in virtual insignificance? Do we begin even where the Australian Labour Party began a couple of years ago, in an absolute defeat? No, we do not begin where any of those parties began, and we do not begin, either, where our party began and restarted on previous occasions in this century in the wake of defeat. In our alliance with the trade unions, in our strength in local government to be used to resist the attacks both on local democracy and on local standards of care and opportunity, in the fact of our determination and in the opportunities for democratic organisation and democratic expression inside and outside parliament, we have assets never known to so many labour and socialist movements in the world. Indeed – unprecedented, for most of our existence, even in this country.

From this conference this week, it is obvious that in the wake of defeat we build not despondency but determination. And we are going to need all of that determination and coherent, persistent unity in order to accomplish the task that we have to. That is now more necessary than ever. It is important for us in our movement, it is imperative for our country.

CONSERVATIVE RECORD

We are ruled by a government whose rhetoric is resolution but whose reality is industrial ruin; whose rhetoric is efficiency, but whose reality is collapse. Their rhetoric is morality, their reality is unemployment which splits and scatters families. An immorality of health cuts which prolong pain; of education cuts that stifle talent; of housing cuts which inflict the misery of crowding and ugliness and homelessness. That is the reality of today's Toryism.

Last week in Canada the prime minister had this to say on the welfare state: 'It might,' she said, 'end up not succouring but suffocating.' And then she said: 'Energy is sapped, initiative is stifled, enterprise is destroyed.' I ask, before the witness of Jack Jones and his new national brigade – as he once belonged to the international brigade – I ask before their witness: are senior citizens in Britain being suffocated by a pension from November of £34.50p a week? I ask: are the seven million of our countrymen and women in poverty being suffocated by their supplementary benefits? I ask if the young people who in this country are lucky enough to get on the Youth Training Scheme are being suffocated by the paltry £25 a week? Are their unemployed contemporaries being suffocated by the £15 and £16 and £17 a week, soon to be cut, according to the government? I say that these people are not being suffocated by care; they are being smothered by neglect, by the contempt of a cruel government.

Because this is a conference of the people, we heard in the last couple of days from Tom Sedden who finished his speech by saying to me as leader of the Labour Party: 'Your job is to get me a job.' I say: 'Yes, Tom, that is a good definition of my job'. We heard from Tony

Hughes yesterday, driven to utter dementia by the awful experience of unemployment, recovering from it because of his strength and the strength of his friends and the family who love him – not because of Margaret Thatcher who considers that any degree of civilised support is suffocation for Tony Hughes.

I recall another person in danger of suffocation who I met on Sunday morning, an eighteen-year-old from Brighton – yes, prosperous Brighton – a sixth-form student doing physics, maths and economics. Do you know what he does? He works for three hours a night cleaning tables so that he can keep himself at sixth form college, so that his talents will be available to the people of this country. But Margaret Thatcher would say that we would suffocate that youth if we were to pay in order that he did not have to work. There is a different morality about Toryism, a different perception of efficiency.

Mrs Thatcher is fond of hoping that her place in history will be that vacated by Winston Churchill. Far be it for me to stand on this platform, especially as a South Walian, and offer any great plaudits to the late Sir Winston Churchill. But everything is relative, you know, and it was Churchill who started off the wage boards which Margaret Thatcher is now intent upon destroying. It was Winston Churchill who, in the memorial speech for David Lloyd George, spoke of the way in which he was glad – I use his word – to be the lieutenant of David Lloyd George as they 'drove the vultures of utter ruin from the dwellings of the nations'. Churchill said: 'Social insurance, the stamps we lick, the roads we travel, the system of progressive taxation, are the principal remedies that have been used against unemployment,' and he gloried in the fact that he was there at the foundation of the welfare state. How does Margaret Thatcher dare to glory in the fact that she is contriving the termination of the welfare state?

It is going to get worse. The government is fixated by their need, self-imposed, to cut a further £2.5 billion in next year's budget. Yesterday it was reported that Michael Heseltine had protected defence expenditure against cuts and now that means that the whole £2.5 billion cut will be taken in unemployment benefits, supplementary benefits, cuts in local government, in education, in social services, in urban aid and in health spending, health cuts. From a government that even promised its own conference this time last year that the health service was 'safe in their hands'. Can the unemployed doctors and nurses believe that the health service is safe in Tory hands? Can communities faced by hospital closures believe it? Can the housewife brought out of anaesthetic on the operating table because the hospital did not have operating theatre clothes, can she believe that the health service is safe in Margaret Thatcher's hands? Can anybody? Can anybody believe it when all around there is evidence of pain being prolonged, of disease being untreated, because a health service that has never been generously funded is now being cut as never before.

Under Toryism, pain is an economic necessity; that is the only conclusion that can be drawn from the scale and the nature of the cuts that are now being inflicted on the National Health Service. I do not want to bring personalities into it, so that means I can talk about Norman Fowler. He made two statements in the course of one week last month – there is Tory productivity for you. In the first, on the Monday, he announced that people could not expect the general practitioner service to be expanded simply because there was more demand for it. So much for demand and supply economics. In other words, people need not expect treatment because they were sick.

The same week, on that Wednesday, he published a further circular to the health authorities urging them to sell facilities to the private sector. Those statements sum up the Tory attitude to the health service. Cut the service to the patient, but fatten the profit of the private contractor and contrive by every means to make that profit bigger and even more diverse. If cuts forbid admission to hospital, or if access becomes dependent upon the ability to pay and people cannot pay, well, then there is always good old Victorian values to fall back on. The sick can stay at home, they can nestle in the compassion and love of relations, not because that is the voluntary obligation accepted by the relations and friends, but because that is the enforced domestication which is the consequence of Tory economic and health policies. That is what their system means, and it does not take any account of whether the family needs to work, whether the wife or the husband can actually stay at home; it does not take any account of the accommodation in the house, whether it means an ageing parent desperately, possibly terminally, ill in the front room, whether it means crowding for the children in the bedrooms – it does not take any of those things into account. Because although all of the effects of these economies, so-called, are on real people, they are made by people who do not understand the needs of real people in our country.

And while all that is going on, I read in the last couple of days of a place in Harley Street, a cell revitalisation clinic. Doctors, presumably trained to a high level of skill at public expense, of course, are injecting monkey cells into the ageing rich in order to rejuvenate them. A very, very complex process. It is obviously failing with the Tory Cabinet although, perhaps that is a bit unfair to the monkeys that gave up their cells.

THE CASE FOR HIGHER PUBLIC SPENDING

I have got a much more satisfactory and simple way of rejuvenating people without all the magic of modern medicine. Rejuvenate people by giving them pensions that are capable of meeting heating costs, just as a start. Rejuvenate them by giving them transport at a price they can afford, and with a frequency they can depend upon to free them from isolation. Rejuvenate them by giving them medical services to free them from pain. Rejuvenate them by giving them home helps and housing to release them from the dreadful anxiety that old people encounter in this country. Yes, rejuvenate them by giving them safe streets to walk on. That is the rejuvenation that we want and it does mean that we have to be unremitting in our defence of the services of what could become known as rejuvenation – public services, local government services, health services.

That defence of those services is a national duty that does not only apply to this movement. I make the appeal to all the people of this country, no matter what they voted on June 9, no matter what they now intend to vote in the next general election or whether they intend to vote at all. Join with us in the defence of a basic, fundamental, essential health service without which this country ceases to be civilised.

As a subscription to that, I begin tomorrow my period of leadership by writing a letter to the prime minister demanding that in the government's time and as quickly as possible after parliament resumes – which, in my book, means hours rather than days – that we have a full scale debate on the health cuts announced during the parliamentary recess. We want to use the national forum of this country, parliament (which is the major weapon of democratic socialism, as it has always been the major weapon of democracy) in order to expose the full extent of the harm and the full extent of the contempt which the government shows towards the health service and the people, all of us, who depend upon that health service. We shall use it for that means.

When we make those demands in parliament in a few weeks time, we know what response we shall get from the government. When we make the demands for the extra resources necessary, they will tell us that the country cannot afford it. They say that the country cannot afford to sustain health expenditure; they say it cannot afford to sustain education expenditure; school meals expenditure, school book expenditure, university and polytechnic places; it cannot afford to maintain railways or cannot afford to maintain housing.

We cannot afford it, they tell us, until the country is more efficient. So, what are they doing to increase efficiency? Is it efficiency that drives industrial output down by 12 per cent in four years? Is it efficiency that drives manufacturing investment down by 30 per cent in four years? Is it efficiency which allows £10,000 million in desperately needed investment capital to leave this country in every one of the last four years? Is it efficiency to contrive that for the first time in British history – not this decade, not since the war, not this century, but for the first time in British history – this manufacturing, producing, trading nation is actually buying more manufactured goods from abroad than we are selling to the rest of the world? Is that efficiency?

I do not call it efficiency. I say it is a sell-out of a country by the government of a country; if you really want a short word for that term, it is a grand scale act of profound economic treachery. That is what they are doing to our country. I'll show you the full hypocrisy and stupidity. Mrs Thatcher is fond of saying you cannot spend what you do not earn. That begins as a fallacy. For, if it was true that you could only spend what you could earn, all of the system that lives by borrowing and lending, the capitalist system, would collapse overnight if we could only spend what we earn. But, also, Thatcherism omits the much more accurate but equally simple fact of the matter in a modern economy. It is not that you cannot spend what you do not earn, but it is the fact that you cannot earn what others do not spend. The fact is that if people are denied the means of spending by deliberate suppression of their standards of living – by the deliberate creation of unemployment, by the deliberate multiplication of the numbers on short-time working, by the withdrawal of over-time pay and production bonuses – they spend less, they demand less. There is then less requirement for the produce of others; when that occurs, there is less work for others to undertake. That is the fact.

We say: 'Why can we not afford decent services?' They say it is because we are not producing enough. We say: 'Why are we not producing enough?' The men of commerce who know all about these things say that it is not really worth it because there is no point, no one is buying. Then we say: 'Why are they not buying?' And they say it is because they cannot afford it. That is the modern tale of Toryism, and they are repeating history as a tragic farce – because we have been here before.

When we make demands they say we cannot afford it because of the world slump. Those who complain most and use it most as an alibi, this word slump, are precisely those who are imposing massive debt burdens and increased interest charges on the very countries whose demand, whose consumption, could be dragging this world out of slump. Do you know, they are so stupid now, this government and their confederates in the International Monetary Fund, that they are ensuring that even where Third-World countries gain additional revenues by increased sales or by higher prices of their raw materials, or by both, they cannot spend the extra revenue on buying our produce in the industrial world – because they are too busy using it up paying that interest. That is the insanity, and that is how poverty becomes a raging world infection.

I would like to make the appeal of decency for the nurturing of the interests of the Third World. I would like to make the appeal on grounds of humanity alone for the Third World to be assisted. Anyone who has seen the skeletons of starvation, who has watched a child of seven years of age weighing less than two stone, should not have to be appealed to. But, if that does not commend itself to people in this, and other, prosperous countries, I say to them: the only way in which we recover from slump in those industrial lands is by ensuring that our fellow human beings right across this world have the means at their disposal of buying our produce.

They say they cannot afford it – they have higher priorities, priorities like Trident. They say that we have got to have Trident, we have got to have nuclear arms, because human nature is such that if you do not have a big stick to hit back with then you will get hit. I will tell you this about human nature; if it really is as the Tories say it is and want it to continue to be, and if it goes to its logical conclusion, this vain, violent human nature that they accept, there is not going to be any human nature left – because there will be no human beings left. That is the fact of their system.

They say we cannot afford it – 'cannot afford', it is not much wonder. If they are so reducing our wealth-producing base by colliery closures, by steel contraction, by selling off our assets – yes, our assets – in British Petroleum, and allowing North Sea oil, this magnificent bonus, to be sopped up by the expenditure on unemployment instead of using it to revitalise our economy, it is not much wonder that we cannot afford. People have been complaining about the way in which farmers are burning straw. I am glad they are complaining about it. Perhaps it will remind them that that is what the Tory government has been doing to the whole economy for the last four years. We have a scorched-earth economy in Britain now because of the way in which they have been misconducting our affairs.

This labour movement can rescue this country because we are willing to invest, we are willing to spend, we are willing to protect, we are willing to control the outflow of that precious capital. We will do it, yes, to gain the advancement and advantages of socialism. But if anybody is actually a little bit timid about that, let me commend to them an old capitalist maxim – 'you have got to spend some to make some'. And if that is true for capitalism, then it certainly is true for a country being driven to its knees by a capitalist government that has not got the sense to understand that if they do not stimulate, expand and spend, then our country becomes totally de-industrialised.

THE LIBERAL/SDP ALLIANCE
Only we can perform that rescue – by the combination of our expenditure, and the fact that we plan to get the maximum advantage out of that expenditure, that we very much do want value for money, because it is our money. There is no one here or, indeed, throughout the vast working classes, those who depend solely upon the sale of their labour, who will shift their money in order to demonstrate their patriotism – who will take it across the currency boundaries in order to get a fast buck, whose greatest commitment is to a profit margin. The people of whom we speak, to whom we speak, the British people, have this country as their own. They invest their lives in it, they want it to be nourished and developed, and I say to them that we are the only party with that similar scale of commitment to permit that nourish-

ment to take place. Others will not do it. Not the Tories certainly; neither will that Alliance, the Liberal/Social Democratic Alliance, the LSD Alliance, the new political hallucinatory drug alliance.

On economic policy (as they have proved), on defence policy, on welfare policy – they are not an alternative to Thatcherism, they are a replica of Thatcherism. That is the Social Democratic–Liberal Alliance. They are bringing true the prophecy of one of their members, Mrs Shirley Williams, who spoke of a party with no roots, no principles, no philosophy, no values. She could have added no members, because finding an SDP activist is a little less likely than finding Lord Lucan wandering around the streets.

There is supposed to be this great bond, this great Alliance. I will tell you what the Alliance is: David Steel tolerates it for as long as David Owen does not absolutely and permanently forbid the prospect of a merger. David Owen tolerates it for as long as David Steel does not absolutely insist upon the prospect of a merger. That is not an alliance, it is a coagulation of convenience. It is not an alliance, it is clotting; that is what that SDP/Liberal relationship is. Anyone not understanding that should have listened, as I did, to the radio programme *World at One*, on September 19 during the Liberal Party conference. Asked by the interviewer about the Alliance, a Liberal rank and filer – you know, these noble creatures – said that it was great, it was marvellous in the election: 'On the doorstep, if anyone had doubts about the SDP, I was a Liberal. If anyone had doubts about the Liberals, I put my SDP badge on.' Now, you know, there is not a substance of conscience, let alone a substance of policy, that is fit to address itself to the great needs of our country.

CONCLUSION

When we make demands we are told to be realistic. I wholeheartedly agree. I think that we have got to be realistic all the time. I have had enough of visionaries like Keith Joseph and Margaret Thatcher. I have had enough of those kinds of dreamers. I have had enough of people who dream that we can have serenity in this world when national greatness is measured in war chests. I have had enough of the dreamers who say that we can endure as a human race when the material resources of this planet are plundered recklessly with no regard for our children's tomorrow. I have had enough of the dreamers who say that we can have the calm and comfort of family life when communities are closed down by mass unemployment. I have had enough of dreamers who think that we can have national pride and national satisfaction when the sick, the old, the poor and the young are ordered to make the major sacrifices to national strength. I have had enough of the dreamers who try and tell us that, with proportional representation and the smiling promise of painless progress, nice people without a rooted value or a chromosome of loyalty between them, can meet and master the demands of our age, when they could not even stand the heat of losing an argument in the party that gave them everything they have got.

I have had enough of those dreamers. Our country, our world, cannot afford them or their mirage that national economic recovery can come from mass bankruptcy; their fantasy that economic prosperity can come out of imposed penury; their idiotic tomfoolery that liberty can result from the fear spread by unemployment and insecurity. I will not take their mirage, their vision, their fantasy and neither should any rational, sane, mature adult of voting age in this country.

These are days for realists. Realists who know that we must produce our way out of slump or we do not get out of slump; realists who know that such production needs investment and demand or we do not get such recovery; realists who require efficiency in the use of resources and not the massive costs of the disuse of people and capital; realists who want rewards for merit instead of privileges for those who inherit; realists who face the technological revolution with training and education to meet its needs and use its proceeds; realists who understand that patriotism is not an empty, clanging replay of the past but the belief in the people of the present and in their potential for the future; realists who will not accept the delusion of great power status or the ruinous risks and costs that go with it. Realism, that is what is needed in this country to save this country, the realism of democratic socialism.

That is the patriotism that I feel in my blood and in my bones. In my brain, in my heart, I know that that is the kind of patriotism that the people of this country really feel – a patriotism of peace, a patriotism of care, a patriotism of justice, of liberty; of competence, yes; of efficiency, yes. That is today's patriotism and this Labour movement is made up of today's people, who borrow nothing from nostalgia, whether for the 1950s and 1960s or for the 1920s or the 1820s. Today's policies for today's people with that patriotism that is betrayed by the despotism of unemployment; patriotism that is betrayed by the withdrawal of educational opportunity, by the reckless waste of oil revenues; patriotism that is betrayed by the war being conducted against local democracy by this Tory government. And when those who prate blimpish patriotism, in the mode of Margaret Thatcher, are also the ones that will take millions off the caring services of this country. I wonder they do not choke on the very word patriotism.

They are the enemy: they must be defeated, and we must defeat them together. If we try by groups and factions, we will not do it. If we give greater attention to arguments between ourselves than to our enmity against them, we will not do it. If we give more attention to impressing each other than convincing the people we have to convince, we will not do it. They are the enemy. They must be defeated and we must defeat them together. That is our purpose. There must be no activity in this Labour movement that is superior to that purpose. Now, and for all time in the future, that is our business. Let us get to it.

1984
BLACKPOOL

'I damn violence – all violence'

By the autumn of 1984 Labour was no longer trailing as far behind the Conservatives as in June 1983. In elections to the European Parliament in June 1984, Labour won 36.5 per cent of the vote in Great Britain, compared with the Conservatives' 40.8 per cent. Labour almost doubled its representation, from seventeen to thirty-two members, while Conservative representation was reduced from sixty to forty-five. (The Liberal/Social Democratic Alliance won 19.5 per cent support, but no seats; one seat was won by the Scottish Nationalists.)

In London, four Labour Greater London councillors had resigned their seats in order to fight by-elections as part of Labour's campaign against the abolition of the GLC. All four won comfortably, although their actions had no perceptible impact on the Government, which finally disbanded the GLC in 1986.

In his speech Kinnock referred to both the European election and the GLC by-elections – but made no reference to another contest: the Chesterfield by-election in March, which saw Tony Benn's return to the House of Commons. (Benn had been defeated at Bristol East in the 1983 general election.)

Two trade union issues preoccupied the Labour Party. The first was the Government's decision to ban trade union membership at the Government's Communications Headquarters (GCHQ) at Cheltenham. Sir Geoffrey Howe, the Foreign Secretary, maintained that the ban was necessary for reasons of national security. Labour and the trade unions argued that the government was violating civil liberties. Although only a small number of workers were involved, the GCHQ trade union ban became an issue of great symbolic importance. The Government had introduced a series of laws requiring unions to act more democratically, and had promoted these laws as enhancing the civil liberties of individual trade unionists. The GCHQ controversy allowed Labour, for once, to respond in kind – and invoke the principle of civil liberties to fight government action.

The second, far larger, issue was the miners' strike. In March, most of Britain's pits stopped work, after the Coal Board had offered a pay rise of 5.2 per cent (the same as the annual inflation rate) and announced a series of pit closures. Arthur Scargill, the president of the National Union of Mineworkers, refused to call a national strike ballot; instead he relied on a series of coalfield ballots.

Nottinghamshire miners decided to continue working. Their decision went far to undermining the strike – which had been called at the end of the winter, and at a time when coal stocks were unusually high. A series of ugly confrontations took place at Nottinghamshire pits, as striking miners (mainly from Yorkshire) manned picket lines to try to bring the pits to a halt. Other confrontations took place at coking plants – notably Orgreave in South Yorkshire, to prevent mined coal from reaching British Steel's Scunthorpe works.

Incidents on picket lines provoked rival accusations – by the police that striking miners were using violence against working miners and the police, and by pickets that the police were themselves using violence to break up their lines. These arguments swiftly engulfed the Labour leadership. Kinnock was challenged repeatedly – first, to denounce Scargill's decision to call a strike without holding a national ballot; and second, to condemn violence by NUM members.

To say that little love was lost between Kinnock and Scargill would be to understate the position. Their relationship was built on loathing and contempt. Scargill regarded Kinnock as a traitor to radical socialism; Kinnock saw Scargill as a dangerous extremist. However, Scargill could not afford to alienate the Labour Party; while within the party few, even those most hostile to Scargill, wanted to say anything critical of the striking miners as a group.

In his speech, Kinnock trod carefully. Invited to condemn violent pickets, he condemned all violence, widening the term to include 'the violence of despair . . . the violence of long-term unemployment . . . the violence of loneliness, decay, ugliness and fear'. He then accused Thatcher of double standards. As for Scargill – Kinnock sidestepped the problem of whether to be falsely nice or bravely nasty. He chose not to mention the miner's president at all. For the moment, Kinnock decided neither to question nor to endorse the tactics of the NUM leadership, or its decision to call a strike without first holding a national ballot. His public judgement on these matters would have to wait until after the strike.

In his speech, Kinnock also sidestepped another tricky issue: plans to overhaul the party's constitution. Following the practice of many local parties (and trade unions), which balloted individual members in the 1983 leadership election, Kinnock wanted to extend the principle of one-member-one-vote to the selection of parliamentary candidates. The National Executive proposed a constitutional amendment of staggering modesty: if passed, it would allow – not force – local parties with sitting MPs to make their reselection decisions by one- member-one-vote ballots. The new rule would not apply to constituencies without a Labour MP – nor to Labour constituencies which did not want to use the new procedure. However, even this slight extension of party democracy met with fierce resistance; the executive's proposal was defeated, on a card vote, by 3,992,000 to 3,041,000.

This vote was taken the day before Kinnock's speech. It demonstrated that Labour's leader was not yet fully master in his own house. Further evidence of this came on the day following his speech. A number of Labour councils were attempting to resist government limits on local spending. Some proposed a strategy of setting illegal budgets, in which services would be maintained while rates were held down. Their hope was that the government would not dare to let councils descend into chaos or bankruptcy, and would eventually relent. Kinnock believed that this strategy would be doomed to fail – and, moreover, it was wrong in principle for elected politicians to flout the law. In his speech, Kinnock did not refer directly to this dispute. However, he did make his views clear when he insisted on the principle of legality and scorned the idea of a 'political "Charge of the Light Brigade"'.

The next morning Liverpool's Derek Hatton proposed a resolution which asked the Conference to support 'any councils which are forced to break the law as a result of the Tory government's policies'. The executive wanted this resolution to be remitted – that is, to be referred to the executive without a vote being taken. However, Hatton insisted on a vote and the resolution was carried on a show of hands.

Kinnock remained convinced that time would prove him right both about the folly of the miners' strike and the futility of law-breaking by local councils. But in his 1984 conference speech he chose to reserve his definitive comments on both matters, and accept the risk that in the short term his right-wing enemies would charge him with cowardice in the face of left-wing extremism.

PK

FOR US it has been a year of advance. Twelve months ago we came to this conference licking our wounds in defeat. We stood at 24.5 per cent in the opinion polls; we were stunned by our worst post-war election defeat.

The commentators, with all of the insight and foresight for which they are famous – at least among each other – were talking about us in deathbed terms. Now, in 1984, we have made great gains in the European Parliament elections, and in the local government council elections in the Spring of this year. In the four GLC by-elections, which our party correctly called, Labour scored huge victories and – more important, in many ways – we completely vindicated our belief in using democracy to try to defend democracy, in London and everywhere else.

That in anybody's book should be strong evidence of substantial and sustained recovery, and it is. Only one thing could possibly arrest that recovery; amnesia, memory loss. It is an awful affliction for anyone, but for a political party it can be an absolutely crippling disease. Indeed, a political party cannot afford any degree of infection by amnesia. It must vaccinate itself completely against such an event. It cannot afford any loss of memory. And in this party, the vaccine is simply to recall what defeat felt like last year, and that should immunise each and every one of us completely against any attitude or activity that can impede our progress towards victory.

All of you who have been winning those European, local and by-elections, know the great feeling of taking an extra pace towards the victory we must achieve at the next election. That is how it has been in this Labour Party, and that is how it must go on: with patience, with understanding, with persuasion, with co-operation, with campaigning, with hard work. Turning outwards, listening to people, and learning from them. Working for the people, working with the people. That is the way the Labour Party will win the election.

The prize for that effort is great: it is the democratic power that we need to save our country. And the prize is there for us to win. Think about it: we have to advance as much in three years as we already have in one year. That is the knowledge that spurs our effort, that gives us confidence and sets our course for victory.

Every month that passes increases the need for that victory. For in this year, whilst we have been building recovery, our country has been pushed further into slide and shambles by the government elected in June of 1983:

- In this year in which the government kept on telling us that the economy is recovering, unemployment has risen by 125,000.
- In this so-called year of recovery, an extra 350,000 young people under twenty-five find themselves unemployed for more than a year.
- In this year of recovery 91,000 more manufacturing jobs have been lost, to add to the 1.7 million manufacturing jobs lost since 1979.
- In this year interest rates went up by a third and mortgage rates soared to 12.5 per cent as the government further applied the very policies that brought the pound tumbling in the first place.
- In this year industrial production has stagnated – fewer cars and commercial vehicles, steel and ships have been produced in this country than in the previous year.

This was a year when our trade deficit in manufactured products – in this country of makers and traders, that for all the foreseeable future must try to live by selling the things that it makes for the rest of the world – doubled to a rate of over £4,000 million. As for the so-called sunrise industries, we heard this year that in Britain the sunrise industry of information technology is being eclipsed before it has properly risen.

These are the statistics of slump, and not the records of recovery. I register them with misery – for our people are the victims of that shrivelling economy. I wish with all my heart that it was true that we were experiencing a recovery – even Mrs Thatcher's recovery. For there is no profit, no comfort, no joy for us in this Labour movement in the drudgery, poverty, despair, and insecurity of anybody's unemployment.

- This was the year, too, when tax was introduced on fish and chips; and, in an industry with over 400,000 unemployed, tax was introduced on home improvements.
- This was the year when farmers slaughtered milk cows.
- This was the year when old age pensioners were charged for their spectacles and lens replacements.
- This was the year when the health service – 'safe in their hands' – was squeezed into further closures and contractions.
- This was the year when the school class-sizes stopped falling; when university admissions kept on falling; when medical and technological research was cut back by the government because of its cuts.
- This was the year in which Cruise arrived. This was the year in which the cost of Trident soared past £12,000 million.
- This was the year when cuts pushed public and local services below the level of legality, while simultaneously government threatened prison to those who tried to spend to keep services up to the levels of decency and service to the community.
- This was the year when the elections for the Greater London and metropolitan county councils were abolished. Why? Because the results would be politically embarrassing and devastating for the government.
- This was the year when the government banned trade unions at GCHQ, Cheltenham. Why? In order to demonstrate its view that security, patriotism, commitment to the national interest, is incompatible with trade unionism. What vile rubbish, utterly unacceptable in any democracy.
- This was the year when Sarah Tisdall went to jail with a punishment vastly in excess of anything that was merited by the offence.
- This is the year when Clive Ponting is on trial and being prosecuted by the government.
- This was the year when national policing was introduced in Britain.
- This was the year in which young mothers were refused help with maternity costs, and families were denied help with funeral bills, because the fathers of those families were on strike.
- This is the year when soup kitchens came back to Britain: 1984, the fifth year of Thatcherism.

MINERS' STRIKE

For seven months of this year, all of those elements – the erosion of civil rights; the withdrawal of welfare support; the cutbacks and closures; unemployment and civil disorder – have all been brought together in a great turmoil of the miners' dispute. That turmoil is the product of Thatcherism – the combination of ignorance and arrogance, of pride and prejudice, that now rules and overrules this country and makes Britain in this fifth year of Thatcherism less free, less fair, less productive than it was for years before 1979.

The erosion of our economic standards, our standards of liberty, of compassion, of care, and of opportunity; it is all that which is, of course, part of the reason for this dispute. Families and communities in the coalfields, like those in my constituency in South Wales, know that pit closures would trap them, entomb them, in unemployment and deprivation for all of the foreseeable future under Toryism. They know that under Thatcherism no alternatives exist and no alternatives are coming to their areas. That is why the resistance has been so determined. People who do not comprehend it should understand that the communities now engaged in this dispute are like someone fighting for air to breathe. That is literally the case under Margaret Thatcher.

Let everybody be clear. This dispute was caused by the fact that the National Coal Board wanted to impose production targets on the industry which would in this year, by the Spring of 1985, bring the closure of twenty pits, the loss of 20,000 jobs, and the reduction of output by four million tonnes – and that was just for starters. They said that the cutback was to bring production into line with the market for coal – that was the phrase they used; they said that the closures were necessary to save £350 million – that's what they said.

As it happens, that programme could not have benefited Britain in any event. In Britain's coalfields now, the male unemployment rates are 15, 18, and 20 per cent. There are no jobs for redundant coal miners to go to. That is the simple, sour fact. And that means that closures would simply turn producers of coal who pay taxes into producers of nothing who have to claim benefits. That's the loss we would be making. It would cost the country more; the whole scheme would, to coin a phrase, be 'uneconomic' for Britain. Even apart from that plain argument of arithmetic, the fact is that this dispute itself has torn the purposes claimed by the Board for their cutbacks and closure programme into absolute ribbons.

Since the Board tried to impose those demands early this year, there has been a seven-month dispute which has cost the country a minimum of nearly £2,000 million in extra oil-burn, in lost taxes, in lost production and in policing costs. Since those demands were made by the Board early this year, there has been a seven-month dispute and fifty-four million tonnes of coal production has been lost. I want this conference, the whole country, and the government to get hold of the facts that the loss of coal production in this dispute is fourteen times more than the loss originally required by the NCB. I want the whole country to get hold of the fact that the financial costs of continuing the dispute are six times as great as any so-called savings that were anticipated from the programme of closures and contractions.

If people understand that, they will comprehend that those are the unrelenting facts which would now persuade the Board and the government to get away from their stupidity and their inflexibility, from their vanities and their posturing, and step out of their 'B' movie script, and act like responsible people and go back to the arrangements before the compilation of the hit-list. That is the pre-condition, the basic requirement, of saving this country and the coalmining communities and much else, from the awful pain of the continuation of this dispute. The government and the Board should get back to the system, and restore confidence in the system of negotiation about exhaustion, which has stood the industry in good stead for many years. They should understand that the National Union of Mineworkers has been prepared to make its case for new investment, and new development of workable reserves, when pits were reported as exhausted. They should remember that, on those grounds of foreseeable and acknowledged exhaustion, agreement had already been made before the dispute started, between the NUM and the NCB, to close about a dozen pits in the next two or three years.

They should revise their coal investment strategy to improve existing pits capable of development, and stop the distortion whereby eight-tenths of investment is going into a small number of coalfields, including pits that will not even produce coal for the next ten years. And, in Mrs Thatcher's case, she should stop saying about the miners, as she said to the *Financial Times*: 'Some of their arguments apply just as much to exhausted pits as to uneconomic ones. If you listened to their arguments [though I never know when she did] you would go on producing mud to keep a community going.'

She ought not to have said things like that, because it only demonstrates her crass ignorance of miners and her gross misunderstanding of the issues in this dispute. There is not a miner who wants to take the purposeless risks of working an exhausted pit or a seam that is anywhere near to such uselessness. There are other occupations devoted to provide fruitless fripperies, and Mrs Thatcher may be used to them and paying exotic prices charged in those occupations; but they don't include coal mining.

The fact is that there is no rational, financial, technical, economic or market reason for the Board and the government to keep the dispute going. Mrs Thatcher has no rational economic case for maintaining the dispute. She has no case based on costs; she has no case based on savings – no rational case. But she does have an irrational purpose in continuing the dispute; it is the purpose of political vanity on a manic scale. And she can only sustain that cause by uproar. That is all she has left now. That is the game.

We must not play the game; we never have; we never will. It is their game not ours. They have used it through the ages. They have always created the conditions of disorder and then sought political credit out of the use of force against that eruption. It is fifty years or more since they did it last. Fifty years in which people thought those days had gone for ever; fifty years in which another kind of Toryism which remembered the conflict and chaos of that system actually refused to operate that tactic.

Now there is a different Toryism: one that is empty of all of the subtle and genteel concern; one that is devoid of consensus values; one that has no compassion, no instinct for conciliation. It is a Toryism that is all spite, bile and arrogance; it is a Toryism exhumed from the past – a Toryism led by an historical throwback, Margaret Thatcher.

Ask the assorted retired senior civil servants; ask one or two bishops; ask the odd judge or two who in an assortment of statements (some with great salvos of publicity, others more subtly) are demonstrating that right across this society – yes, from the men and women struggling in the coalmining communities now, up to the lords and judges and all stations and classes and ages and sexes in between – the comprehension is growing of the nature of the government that is ruling this country.

The fact that she is tearing the society apart is therefore increasingly obvious; but perhaps what is less obvious is that it is exactly what Mrs

Thatcher promised to do. This conference didn't need warning. This party tried to warn people. They thought we were exaggerating; they thought we were simply engaging in the partisan knock-about; they thought we were just trying to frighten people. There are millions in this country now who wished they had heeded our lessons, and understood that Thatcherism is a personal fixation turned into a system of government.

That is the state of affairs. And in all economic policy, in all social policy, in their very appearance and their conduct of government, this government creates the climate of confrontation, the conditions of conflict: it speaks only the language of conquest. And, in the midst of all of that chaos, in the midst of all that assault on the essentials of civilised life in this country and of values of this country, they call for the condemnation of violence.

I do not respond to that, because it is a taunt, a call to forswear intimidation from a government that bases its whole policy on intimidation. I do condemn violence. I condemn the violence of despair; I condemn the violence of long-term unemployment; I condemn the violence of loneliness, decay, ugliness, and fear. I condemn the violence done to hope, the violence done to talent, the violence done to family security and family unity. I condemn the violence done to civil and personal rights in this country.

I condemn the violence, too, of the stonethrowers and the battering-ram carriers. And I condemn the violence of the cavalry charges, the truncheon groups, and the shield bangers. I condemn violence, I abominate violence, I damn violence – all violence. All violence, without fear or favour. That's what I do and that is what makes me different from Margaret Thatcher. I don't have her double standards. I do not take her selective and blinkered view of conflict.

Of course, I do take sides in this dispute. I couldn't do otherwise with my background. But in any case, even if I didn't come from where I came from, I would find the case for coal compelling, and the case for the communities overwhelming. So I take sides in this dispute; this movement takes sides in this dispute. But the only side I am prepared to take when it comes to violence, is to oppose it. The prime minister should do the same thing, instead of delighting in turmoil and using the police as a replacement for policy.

Yes, that she is doing, and the police know it too. They realise that they are being made into the 'meat in the sandwich'. They realise the pressures are on them to make them depart from the most basic, resilient and most orderly value of British policing – the feeling that they have that they are citizens in uniform. They know that pressure is being applied by the government to make them move away from that tradition; and they also know what the cost, the bitter cost, of being the 'meat in the sandwich' will be. We will be paying that cost for a very long time to come in many of the mining communities.

SOCIALISM, DEMOCRACY AND LEGALITY

In our society on every side we see things being torn apart. We see terrible wrongs done to the young and the old, we see wrongs done to the poor and the disabled; we see industries decimated, communities deprived, liberties lost. We see unjust laws – laws which are nothing more than prejudice made statute. And every fibre rages against the injustice and the waste of all that. And we ask ourselves; what we can do about it? For socialists that is the question of the ages – because it is in our very nature, in our conviction, that we want to do something. Especially when we are faced by injustice. It was a question faced by our movement in the 1930s; and they came back with the answer that the democratic road was the only route for British socialism. All other options, they said, were closed since socialism by insurrection was pure fantasy, and socialism without the ballot box would simply never secure the support and understanding of the British people. They were right. They were right in times even more dangerous than ours, when fascism was pressing on every gate of liberty. Democracy is the first premise of our socialism; it is a matter of principle, not of convenience; it is a matter of commonsense, not of tactics.

With its absolutism, its dogmatism, its controls on local councils, its destruction of opportunities, its war on trade unionism, it is Toryism which defaces and relegates democracy in our country – not Labour, or the cause of Labour.

In saying that, we are not being smug and cosy, and giving in for the duration of the Tory government, when we hold to our belief in democracy. We are upholding the only system which can give us power; the only system that we want to give us power; and the only system that we are prepared to wield when we have that power. Democracy is our cause at all times and in every respect. That is not a call to wait in idleness; it is not a call to relax until the election comes along. On the absolute contrary, it is a call to action – action to

65

articulate and publicise the complaint of the people, for if they cry quietly, they will cry alone; action to break through the indifference to the scandals of social deprivation and industrial destruction in this country; action to pressure ministers and promote concessions, action to rouse and rally and resist; action to protect and promote the interest of the people that we are in politics to help; action that is continual; action that recruits and mobilises new people in our cause.

That is the action of democracy. We are democrats. At the earliest possible time we want to pass and enforce laws to redress grievances; to promote justice and opportunity, to punish race and sex prejudice; to change economic ownership and rewards. We want the power of the law to do that – so we cannot sharpen legality as our main weapon for the future, and simultaneously scorn legality because it doesn't suit us at the present time. To recognise that is not to be defeatist. It is to recognise the facts as they exist and as they are supported by the great mass of Labour people and Labour supporters in this country. To recognise that is not to bow down before a vague and variable idea called the 'sanctity of the law', because we all know how that can be built and bent to defend vested interests. It is to acknowledge that our greatest service to those who need our protection and provision from different laws, is to get power and turf out the authors of the present injustice.

We have to work for that incessantly, singlemindedly. It is a great cause but it is a careful and cool-headed cause. The people who need the support and safeguard of trade unionism and of public services, cannot afford to be part of any political 'Charge of the Light Brigade'. There is no glory in defeat for them; there is just nothing but extra miserable burdens of insecurity and insufficiency. In those circumstances, it is they – the poorest, the weakest, and the most needy – who are the martyrs. That's the fact.

THE NEED FOR POWER

Our political mandate to change the Tory laws and conditions arises partly out of the evidence of their injustice. That exposure must be fierce and relentless; and, when we gain that mandate, we will use it with the full rigour of our power to promote fairness and freedom, and to punish those who dodge their taxes, or pay sweatshop wages, or practise racialism, or any of the other evils of our society. We will do that, we will have the right to do it, and we will have the power to do it.

And we will need the power. You see there is not an aspiration listed this week, or any other week, by this Labour movement that will be fulfilled unless we achieve the power of democratic government.

Our ideals inspire, our policies offer the answers; but however much they intrigue us and encourage us, they are adornments, even entertainments, unless we have power to put them into practice. That is the reality. That is what we know. That is the understanding. Grip it like you would grip a weapon, that reality; hold on to it as we work for our election. Understand that we must have power to house the homeless; we must have power to release the poor; we must have power to provide care for the sick, to refashion and extend the National Health Service.

Power to change the balance of power itself, to restore and develop the structure of democratic government in this country – so that local authorities can have real rights, and so trade unionism can have real rights in this country. We need the power to provide girls and women with the full practical entitlements of equality and no less. We need the power to take prejudice and partisanship out of industrial relations and trade union legislation. We need that power to respond to the needs of pensioners, and to give liberty, choice, comfort, and security in old age. We need the power to meet the justified demands of black people; that they shall have personal and economic status that is equal to any of this country's citizens – regardless of their colour or creed. We need the power to provide the full equipment of education and training for our children. We need the power to provide the effective defence of our country and our values, by meeting the obligations of modern conventional defence and of alliance – without nuclear weapons, which by their possession make us a nuclear target and would by their use terminate our existence and all future forms of existence.

We need the power to work for peace and co-existence between East and West and to make it resilient and dependable. We need the power to achieve a new contract between the North and South of this planet, power to ensure that those countries of the Third World do not use up all of their pitiful earnings in debt repayments to the financiers of the industrial countries, but are able to achieve economic progress and freedom by using what they have and what they can be given to sponsor development, and become consumers instead of supplicants.

Most of all, comrades, we want and we need power to operate a full policy for employment. It will not be the full employment conceived in the 1940s. It will not be the re-establishment of a society which is ethically, socially, and economically dependent upon work for over forty hours a week between the ages of sixteen and sixty-five for most people – or, more accurately, for most men. Those days have gone, and they are not coming back. You and I know it, but what we need now is a policy for employment in this decade, and in the 1990s and in the 21st century.

This must have three main elements. First, it must be led by a strategy for investment that means that in the very course of expenditure we add value and strength to our economy. That means investment to use and to develop new technology, so that it is a servant and never a tyrant. It means investing in our economic infrastructure of transportation, communication, construction and energy. Second, it must sponsor the growth of production and demand in order to deliberately generate jobs in our country. Third, it must also decrease the supply of people seeking employment through a shorter working year and a shorter working life.

The tasks of the modern world need extra preparation and we can get it by the comprehensive provision of extended education and training for youngsters, with reasonable pay so that they as individuals, and their country collectively, are better able to conquer the challenges of future employment, future technology, and future development. And at the other end of working life, we need to provide for the gradual, voluntary and systematic reduction in retirement age – both by the provision of proper pensions, and by ensuring that the extra years of leisure are attractive and fulfilling, and not a condemnation to loneliness and semi-poverty.

When people hear that message of a rational way of approaching the real employment, economic and technological requirements of our age, they say: 'Yes, we like that. Sponsor jobs and at the same time reduce the number of people needing to look for jobs in any given generation. We like that.' But, they say: 'Can it happen?'

My answer is: 'It's happening now'. But it is happening in the most clumsy and cruel way. Men and women in their early fifties are now being forced through redundancy into terminating their working life. Nobody asked them if they wanted to; nobody planned it; nobody made additional provision. They are out – and it's happening now. And for the youngsters, over a million under 25-year-olds in our

68

country are out of work and many have never experienced full-time work. Can it happen? they ask. It is happening now, in the worst possible way. Better to civilise it, to turn it, to organise it; to make it supportive to the needs of the people, instead of making that change trample all over the people. That is why our approach is rational.

Then they ask: 'Can we afford it?' I say that we are paying the price now, both in the direct £17,000 billion bills of unwanted idleness, and in the indirect but massive postponed costs of despair, of frustration, of conflict. The rational course is to recognise the change, and then to make it work to the advantage of the people. That is why we are socialists; that is why we seek power – to seek that mastery of change for the benefit of the people. If we don't, we shall see with terrible speed, and with awful results, the irrational response to technological and economic change which the market economy and the social market economy makes, and has always made – huge numbers of unemployed, millions more who live in a constant fear of unemployment and the insecurity which it brings; and an affluent few who are safe in their jobs but in danger everywhere else.

That isn't the society we want. In short we want a new concept. Modern full employment by these means before we allow the advent of an unprecedented scale of mass unemployment. That is not an option which we will tolerate. I'll tell you why I won't tolerate it, in the simplest terms: it is not an option that I am prepared to offer my children, and therefore it is not an option I am prepared to offer anybody else's children, either.

That, above all, is why we need power. Let us in this Labour movement together with the people of this country plan for it carefully. Let us have the courage to make honest choices and practical priorities; let us work for it together. And when we win, let us use that power to keep our promise of liberty and of peace. For that isn't just the way to get power, it is also the way to keep power.

1985
BOURNEMOUTH

'I'm telling you – and
you'll listen'

By the end of September 1985 Labour was in all kinds of trouble. Its support had drifted down towards 30 per cent, despite the government's mid-term woes. Political momentum seemed to lie with the centre rather than the left. For a brief period the Liberal/SDP Alliance took the lead in the opinion polls. They added to their popularity with successful party conferences by the Social Democrats in Torquay and the Liberals in Dundee. Labour delegates gathered in Bournemouth facing the prospect – as they had in 1981 – that they might be relegated to third place, behind both the Conservatives and the Alliance, at the following general election. Labour badly needed to match the Alliance's conference successes, but was impeded by two internal battles between the leadership and the left – over Militant's control of Liverpool City Council; and over the failure of the coal strike, which had collapsed earlier in the year.

When Labour regained control of Liverpool City Council in 1983, only a minority of its councillors were members of the Militant Organisation; but this minority wielded effective power. It decided to confront the government's policies towards local councils. At the 1984 conference the final outcome of this confrontation had been in doubt, and, as we have seen, delegates voted to back a resolution moved by Derek Hatton, Liverpool City Council's deputy leader.

In June 1985, the council set its budget for the year. It increased rates by 9 per cent, and decided to make no cuts in services. This decision challenged government policy in two ways. First, the budget was not set until eleven weeks after the beginning of the financial year; second, the council budgeted deliberately for an illegal deficit. Militant's aim was to provoke a crisis within Liverpool, forcing the government to offer extra aid to the city. Such an outcome (so Militant's ideologues maintained) would demonstrate to working people throughout Britain that revolutionary politics could succeed where parliamentary opposition had failed. Militant stood to gain hugely from such a demonstration; equally, Labour's leadership stood to be humiliated as much as the Conservative government.

Militant's strategy failed miserably. In late August council officials warned Hatton that Liverpool would run out of money to pay staff wages by the end of the year. Under employment legislation passed by the previous Labour government, the council would have to issue ninety-day redundancy notices to all 31,000 employees. Militant saw this requirement as an opportunity to provoke the very crisis it sought. Hatton told the council unions not to worry: in practice all jobs would be safe. But members of three unions – NUPE, NUT and NALGO – feared that their jobs would be at risk. They refused to distribute the redundancy notices. By late September Hatton needed urgently to find an alternative means of distribution. On Friday, 27 September – two days before the start of Labour's conference – he hired a fleet of thirty taxis to deliver the notices to all 31,000 council employees.

This episode fractured the left-wing alliance in Liverpool that Militant needed if it was to retain untrammelled power. By its timing it also ensured that Militant's stewardship of Liverpool would be raised during the Bournemouth conference. Kinnock's choice was to repeat his 1984 formula – proclaim robustly the need for local councils to remain within the law, but not mention Liverpool in terms – or to confront Militant and Hatton directly.

He chose the latter course. His celebrated condemnation of 'the grotesque chaos' of Liverpool city council was the result.

The following morning Kinnock delivered his second speech. He replied on behalf of the national executive to a debate on the miners' strike. Composite motion 69 had been proposed by Arthur Scargill. Its most contentious clause called on 'the next Labour government to . . . reimburse the National Union of Mineworkers and all other unions with all monies confiscated as a result of fines, sequestration and receivership'. In his speech, Scargill said: 'Surely there is a class issue here . . . There is nothing peculiar or strange about introducing retrospective legislation. There is nothing peculiar or strange about giving a commitment to a trade union movement, who find themselves at the wrong end of Tory laws that are clearly designed to attack the basic democracy of unions.' To Kinnock, however, retrospective legislation was wrong in principle and had to be resisted.

This argument divided the conference almost exactly down the middle. The executive's decision to oppose the NUM motion was taken by the narrowest of margins – fifteen votes to fourteen; Kinnock only achieved this result by persuading one executive member, Michael Meacher, to abandon his previous support for the far left and to switch sides. The debate itself was bitter. Ron Todd, general secretary of the transport workers' union, spoke in favour of the motion; three other union leaders – David Basnett (general and municipal workers), Gavin Laird (engineers) and Eric Hammond (electricians) spoke against. Hammond's description of the striking miners provoked uproar. Echoing the German high command's view of the British infantry in the First World War, he said the miners were 'lions led by donkeys'.

At the end of the debate, Kinnock replied. He spoke from notes he had made during the morning, rather than from a prepared text. At the end of his speech, he asked Scargill to remit his motion. Scargill refused. His motion was approved by 3,542,000 to 2,912,000. Like Gaitskell twenty-five years earlier, Kinnock had lost: but Scargill had failed to secure a two-thirds majority for his motion. Under Labour's rules, the policy of making retrospective changes to the law had won too little support to warrant inclusion in Labour's programme.

PK

LEADER'S SPEECH

THIS WEEK in which our Conference meets is the 333rd week of Mrs Thatcher's government. In this average week in Tory Britain 6,000 people will lose their jobs, 225 businesses will go bankrupt, £400 million will be spent on paying the bills of unemployment, 6,000 more people will be driven by poverty into supplementary benefit; in this week in the world at large over $10,000 million will be spent on armaments and less than $1,000 million will be spent on official aid; and in this week over 300,000 children will die in the Third World. These are the real challenges that we have to face, at home and abroad. These are the concerns of our nation; they are the crises of our world. These are the problems which we in our party address and must address this week and every other week. Only we will address them this week and every other week, because that is what our party is for.

The Tories do not see things like that. They do not believe that these are great problems of substance at all. They think that all of the woes are simply a matter of 'presentation', as they put it. Presentation – that is what their ministers tell each other, that is what their Conference will tell itself next week, that is what the Prime Minister uses to explain everything: it is all a matter of presentation. The unemployment does not really exist, the training centres have not been shut down, the Health Service is safe in their hands: it is all just a matter of presentation. Indeed, they are so convinced of that that they have now got rid of Mr John Selwyn Gummer. He has been sent off to the Ministry of Agriculture, where doubtlessly the expertise that he gained as Chairman of the Tory Party in handling natural fertiliser will come in very handy.

In little Selwyn's place we have Mr Norman Tebbit, charged with the task, so the newspapers tell us, of explaining the government to the country. The last person to have that commission was Dr

76

Goebbels. Whilst Lord Willie Whitelaw, so the newspapers tell us, retains responsibility for co-ordinating the presentation of government policy. Norman and Willie – surely arsenic and old lace! Still, to give the devil his due, Mr Tebbit has been very frank about his whole function. A few days ago he said: 'I don't mind being blackguarded for what we've done, but I don't want to be blackguarded for what we haven't done.'

He will not mind then if I ask him to take a little time off from commissioning young Tories to litter the streets of Bournemouth – and give us a few explanations. Ask him to explain, for instance, how the self-acclaimed party of law and order comes to preside over a record 40 per cent rise in crime in our country in the last six years. How does the declared party of school standards contrive a situation in which Her Majesty's inspectors can describe the schooling system as 'inadequate, shabby, dilapidated, outdated', and then on top of that the Government goads the most temperate of professions – the teachers – into taking prolonged sanctions in the schools they work in? How does the party of the family cut child benefit, cut housing benefit, reduce nursery schooling, turn hundreds of women into immigration widows? How does the party of the family hit the old and the sick by cutting funds in the health and social services? How does the party of the family, indeed of the country and the suburbs, isolate the villages and the suburbs by destroying public transport services? How does the party of the family, above all, so arrange things that this year there is the lowest number of public housing starts in the whole of modern history, the same year in which a Prime Minister makes provision for her retirement with a £450,000 fortress in Dulwich? Is that the mark of the family party?

How is it that the party that promised to roll back the state has arrived at the situation where 1,700,000 more people are entirely dependent on the state because of their poverty during the time the Tories have been in government? How can the party of freedom, the friends of freedom, illegalise trade unionism in GCHQ Cheltenham? How can the party of freedom abolish the right to vote in the Greater London and metropolitan county councils? How can the party of freedom prosecute Sarah Tisdall and Clive Ponting? How can the party of freedom make secret plans to surrender completely the sovereignty of the British people in the event of war? How can the party of freedom do that? That did not happen when the Panzer

77

divisions were at the French coast, when this country was in its most dire jeopardy. The institutions of freedom in this country were maintained. We insist that at all times of national gravity, at any time of public jeopardy, there is all the more reason for us to sustain the values and the institutions of our democracy in this country. That is what we tell the party of freedom.

How does the party of enterprise preside over record bankruptcies? How does the party of tax cuts arrange that the British people now carry the biggest ever burden of taxation in British history? And how, above all, does the party that got the power by complaining that 'Labour isn't working' claim in the name of sanity that there is a recovery going on, when unemployment rises remorselessly to the point where this Thursday they will record 3.4 million British people registered unemployed even on their fiddled figures? That is an awful lot – 3.4 million – of 'Moaning Minnies', even for the most malevolent Maggie to try and explain away.

They are the paradoxes, they are the inconsistencies, they are the hypocrisies that Norman Tebbit has got to try and explain. No wonder they have given him a professional fiction writer as deputy chairman. But even if Jeffrey Archer was a mixture of the inventive genius of Shakespeare and Houdini and Uri Geller all rolled up into one, he still would not be able to do the trick, because the British people have rumbled. They have rumbled the methods, the motives, the style of this Government. They now understand. The great majority of the British people, including very much those who are not disadvantaged, are now alarmed and ashamed by the way that this Government rules, the divisions it creates, the dangers that it creates in our country. Their concern is recorded in every opinion poll, it is obvious in the statements of clergymen, it is even apparent amongst the soggier elements of the Conservative Party; and the breadth of that concern is evidence of the breadth of decent values and attitudes among the British people.

The Government ignores those feelings. They propose no concessions, no changes. All we get is a fleeting visit to what the Prime Minister thinks of as 'the far North' and we get a Secretary of State for Employment in quarantine in the House of Lords. The other response that the Government makes to national crisis is to preach continually that there will be some great miracle of prosperity in some great non-unionised, low wage, tax-dodging, low-tech privatised day that one time will come upon us. It is a myth, mirage, fantasy, and the British people now know that. They want a government that changes those policies; they want a government that will lift the poor and the unemployed; they want jobs to be generated; and they have demonstrated in overwhelming majorities that they want unemployment and insecurity to be fought by the Government, not used by the Government as the main tool of its economic policies. That is what the British people want. They resent the Tory strategy of fear. They know that fear brings caution, insecurity breeds stagnation. It does not bring the 'get up and go' society that Mrs Thatcher talks about; it brings the 'keep your head down, hang on to what you've got, stay scared' society. That is what it brings – anxiety. And the penalties of disadvantage do not make confidence or co-operation or strength or stability; they make deference, they make division, they make weakness. Yes, and they make conflict too. When tension, division, distrust, racism and idleness are ignited by hopelessness, all of those policies of fear and neglect create chaos in our society and on our streets.

I say that we cannot afford to be ruled by a government that does nothing to combat that lethal mixture of stagnation and strife. We could not afford it at any time, but least of all can we afford it now, when our society must change or decay. We are in that time now, when there must be a better way to face those challenges, those alternatives, than the way that is shown by the Government of Margaret Thatcher.

THE ROLE OF THE STATE

I believe I know that in this party we do have that better way. I believe we have it because we have the values, the perceptions and the policies that come from democratic socialism. We have the combination of idealism, which stops us throwing in the towel and giving in to the defeatism of Toryism, and the realism which makes us buckle down to finding and implementing the answers. That is the essence of what we believe in. That is the combination of idealism and realism that this country needs now. I say to this movement and I say to the country: that combination is more necessary than ever before.

We live in a time of rapidly and radically changing technology. We live at a time of shifts in the whole structure of the world economy. We live at a time of new needs among the peoples of the world and new aspirations among young people and among women – late but welcome new aspirations among half of humankind. In the light of those changes, we need governing policies in this country that can gain change by consent. That will not come from a government that bullies and dictates. It will not come from a government that evades change and dodges the real issues. Change by consent can only be fostered by a government that will deliberately help people to cope with, handle and manage that change. That is the task for us – to promote change in such a way that it advances the people, all of the people.

Change cannot be left to chance. If it is left to chance, it becomes malicious, it creates terrible victims. It has done so generation in, generation out. Change has to be organised. It has to be shaped to the benefit of a society, deliberately, by those who have democratic power in that society; and the democratic instrument of the people which exists for that purpose is the state – yes, the state. To us that means a particular kind of state – an opportunity state, which exists to assist in nourishing talent and rewarding merit; a productive state, which exists to encourage investment and to help expand output; an *enabling* state, which is at the disposal of the people instead of being dominant over the people. In a word, we want a servant state, which respects those who work for it and reminds them that they work for the people of the country, a state which will give support to the voluntary efforts of those who, in their own time and from their own inspiration, will help the old, the sick, the needy, the young, the ill-housed and the hopeless.

We are democratic socialists. We want to put the state where it belongs in a democracy – under the feet of the people, not over the heads of the people. That is where the state belongs in a democracy. It means the collective contribution of the community for the purpose of individual liberty throughout the community; of individual freedom which is not nominal but real; of freedom which can be exercised in practice because the school is good, because the hospital is there, because the training is accessible, because the alternative work is available, because the law is fair, because the streets are safe – real freedoms, real choices, real chances, and, going with them, the real opportunity to meet responsibilities. It is not a state doing things instead of people who could do those things better; it is not a state replacing families or usurping enterprise or displacing initiative or smothering individualism. It is the absolute opposite: it is a servant state doing things that institutions – big institutions, rich institutions, corporate institutions, rich, strong people – will not do, have not done, with anything like the speed or in anything like the scale that is necessary to bring change with consent in our society. That kind of state is the state that we seek under democratic control.

LIBERAL/SDP ALLIANCE

It cannot be done with brutality and it cannot be done with blandness either. That is why the Social Democrats and the Liberals are utterly useless for the purpose of securing change with consent. They are in Polo politics – smooth and firm on the outside and absolutely nothing on the inside. They do not really do anything or say anything to address the real problems. They have just had a fortnight of conferences, most of which they spent talking about themselves, and having a sort of a seminar about which David was going to play second fiddle, because we all know which David is going to play first trumpet, don't we? They cannot be the enablers, for while there are doubtlessly people in their ranks who seek the decent ends of opportunity and production, there is no one there who will commit the means to secure those ends of opportunity and production. That is in the nature of the attitude that they have.

On top of all that in any case all of their aims for the next election are geared to one objective – a permanent, vested interest in instability, a hung Parliament, in which they can be the self-important arbiters of power. That would be contemptible at any time, but at a time when the Government is going to have to get on immediately, urgently, emergently with the task of generating jobs and investment, a strategy which is intent upon horse trading, juggling, balancing and ego flattering is totally contemptible, and the British people should know that.

JOBS, INDUSTRY AND WELFARE

The Tories meanwhile do not desire enabling ends and plainly will not commit enabling means. In every policy of the Tory government they have shown that their objective is to reduce what we have of an enabling state, what we have of a welfare state, to a rubble of shabby services and lost jobs. Of course they tell us they are not 'real jobs'. Teachers, doctors, nurses, home helps, ancillaries in the schools and in the hospitals, ambulances drivers – they are not real jobs, that is what the Tories tell us. We know they are real jobs. We know they are real jobs because if those jobs are not done, if people are not allowed to do them, the consequence is real pain, real loss of opportunity, real suffering, real misery, yes, and real costs too. That is why they are real jobs, as real as life and death.

We see the Tories' attitude towards enabling people in the education cuts; we see it in the closure of skill centres and training boards; we see it in the reduction in apprenticeships; we see it in the attempted withdrawal of board and lodging allowances to un-employed youngsters and to the chronically sick who need residences. Above all, we now see the Government's attitude towards enabling in the proposals made by Norman Fowler in his social security review, which you debated this morning; 'social security review'.

It would more appropriately be called social insecurity for you and you and you and you. Everybody in this country is going to be disadvantaged if they ever get the chance to implement those policies fully.

In the Labour Party we are fighting, and we will go on fighting, those Poor Law proposals, and as part of that fight early next year we will launch Labour's Freedom and Fairness campaign to put the issue to the British people, to give them our alternatives and to show that once again we have real policies for hope to put in place of fear, which is the only Tory policy. Of course hope is cheap; attractive, delightful, but cheap. Help costs money. So in the course of that fight and in our policies for construction and care we have to take full account of the breadth and depth of the ruin made by the policies of eight or maybe even, by then, nine years of applied Thatcherism. The extent of that ruin is awful. Last Wednesday the Association of British Chambers of Commerce reported.

> *'Our shrinking manufacturing base and deteriorating trade performance raises a fundamental question about the future of the British economy. How do we pay our way in the world when the oil trade surplus, at present a huge £11.5 thousand million, begins to disappear in the late 1980s. Answers to these questions from economic ministers and senior civil servants have been unsatisfactory.'*

Comrades, in the last six years, alone among the major industrial nations, manufacturing production in Britain has actually fallen by 8 per cent; investment in manufacturing production has fallen by 20 per cent; manufactured trade has moved from a surplus of £4,000 million in the last year of the Labour government to a deficit of £4,000 million in the sixth year of the Tory government. In the years since 1979 our economic strength has been eaten away just as surely as if we had been engaged in a war. I put it to this party, I put it to the country, not as a defence, not in any defensive sense whatsoever, but as a salutary fact of life. The Tories have been the party and the government of destruction. If we are to rebuild and recover in this country, this Labour Party must be the party of production. That is where our future lies. It is not a new role for us, but it does require a fresh and vigorous reassertion.

Over the years our enemies and critics – yes, and a few of our friends as well – have given us the reputation of being a party that is solely concerned with redistribution, of being a party much more concerned about the allocation of wealth than the creation of wealth. It was not true, it is not true; it never has been and all our history shows that – from the great industrial development and nationalisation Acts of the Attlee Government, which gave this country a post-war industrial basis, through to the Wilson Government's investment schemes and initiatives that brought new life to where I come from, to South Wales, to Scotland, to the North-East, to Merseyside, to the new towns of the South-East, right through to the actions of the last Labour Government, which ensured that at least we retained a British computer industry, a British motor industry, a machine tool industry, a shipbuilding industry. We have a long record and need give no apology for being the party of production.

Now in the 1980s we face new challenges in our determination that our country shall produce its way out of slump. There is the challenge of the hi-tech industries, which six years ago had a surplus with the rest of the world and now run a £2.3 billion deficit with the rest of the world, as a result of deliberately depressed demand, withdrawal of research and development and expensive money – the policies of the Tory Government. We have challenges too from the traditional industries, those industries dismissed, written off, by a Tory government that calls them 'smoke-stack' industries and really thinks that Britain's future is as a warehouse, a tourist trap, with nothing to export but our capital. That is the vision they have of the future – totally impractical, ruinous, not only for our generation but for all those to come.

Through our Jobs in Industry campaign, in all our policies, we in this party say to the British people: Britain has made it, Britain can make it and, provided that we give to the workers, the managers, the technicians, the people of Britain the means to make it, Britain will make it in the future if we have a Labour government. Those means that they must have at their disposal are training, research and development, and finance for investment over periods and at prices that producers can and will afford. That is absolutely crucial. Other countries do it, and nobody has yet explained satisfactorily to me how it can be, why it should be, that we have a government and a financial system that believe that Britain can't do it, Britain can't make it and in any case Britain shouldn't make it in the future. We cannot afford that surrender mentality from government. We have got to have a government like those of Japan, Germany, Sweden, France and Italy, which put the real interests of their country first. They don't talk about competing in the world economy as if it is a game of cricket. They talk about competing and they mean it, so they put their money where their speeches are.

I am not saying that an economy can revive and thrive only with government; I am saying that it is a fact of life in a modern economy that there can't be any real progress while the policies of a government lie like a great stone across the path of productive manufacturing advance. I am not saying that it can only be done with government; I am saying that the fact of life is that we will not revive and thrive without the active support, involvement, participation of government.

To all those defeatists, the real moaning Minnies of Britain, who say: 'That's all very well, but British workers won't respond, British managers won't respond,' I say: go to the industries in Britain where modernisation has taken place, some of them foreign-owned, and see how, when people have the means, they can stand their corner with any competing industry in the world. I say too to them: go to where, in Labour local authorities, enterprise boards have been established, bringing together public capital and private capital, bringing together people with common objectives, and see how they succeed in measurement by anybody's terms. Go and see, where people get the chance, how they take that chance, how they use it, how they use money to make production, how they spend some to make some, how they are determined to make modern things for modern markets, and do it successfully – from handicrafts right across to the frontier technologies.

We won't accept the defeatism, the surrender mentality. That is why the first priority as the next government of Britain will be to invest in Britain. It has been obvious for decades and disastrously clear since the Thatcher Government took away controls on the export of capital six years ago that Britain is a grossly under-invested country. There is less excuse for that now than ever. The Tories have had more oil money in every month that they have been in government than Jim Callaghan's government had in a whole year of government. They have spent that money on sustaining unemployment, and even as the oil money poured out on that unemployment, even as it poured in to the Exchequer, the investment money poured out of the British economy altogether.

In the last six years over £60,000 million of investment capital has left Britain. *We* need that money – not the Labour Party or the Labour Government: Britain needs that money, if we are to rebuild. That is why we are going to establish our scheme to bring the funds back home where they are needed, so that they can be used for generating employment, development and growth in our economy. We are going to use those funds for long-term loans for the purchase of modern machinery, for research and development, for training. We will ensure that the return paid is comparable to what can be got elsewhere. But the difference will be this: those resources will be here, for the process of investment, for the purpose of creating wealth, for the purpose most of all of generating jobs here in Britain.

We don't make those arguments for getting and using that money out of any jingoistic or nationalistic motive. What we say is this: we need those policies for we simply cannot afford the level of charity shown by the moneyhandlers of Britain towards our advanced industrial competitors. That charity is too expensive for this country to tolerate any longer. We need that money. We need the money to be able to produce; we need the money to be able to generate those jobs, further development, new investment. We need that wealth to reward people for their effort, for their enterprise. And we need that money and the wealth that it generates to provide the means of properly funding the system of justice and opportunity and care which I call the enabling state.

BRITAIN'S OBLIGATIONS TO THE THIRD WORLD
We need that money to make our way in the world, but there are other

ways too in which we must make our way in the world. We must make our way morally as well as economically. For us as democratic socialists there can be no retreat from our duties as citizens of the world. We don't want to be the world's policemen, we don't want to pretend that we are the world's pastor either. But we must be the friends of freedom; and as people who believe that the great privilege of strength, the great privilege of being strong, is the power which it gives to be able to help people who are not strong, we understand where our obligations are in this world.

If the morality won't convince people, if the ethics won't convince people, let the practicalities – the material practicalities – convince them. In this world now we either live together or we decay separately. It is in our material interest to ensure that the supplicants of the Third World are turned into customers and consumers by relieving them of the terrible burdens of interest, by the effectiveness of our aid policies and by assisting in their development. That is a clinical fact stripped of all emotion, and I use it to persuade the falterers. But even to them I say that if you had come with me this year to see the different levels of need in the *barrios* of Managua and the *shambas* of Tanzania, in the desert settlements of Kenya and, most of all, in the back streets of Addis Ababa – for I have never seen such destitution – I would not have to tickle you with profit. If you had seen and touched and felt and smelt, you would know where your duty as free people, as people with money, as people with power and strength, really lies in this world. I say to those people that they would want to do all they could to give life and to help people make a life for themselves. They would. That is what the British people showed just on the basis of television pictures, even without the touch on the skin of a starving child. The British people showed it, and will go on showing that they feel that putting food in people's stomachs and putting clothes on people's backs and putting roofs over people's heads is our place in the world; and, even more than that, they show they understand that helping people to provide the means to grow their food, to make their clothes, to find their freedom, is our place in the world in this democracy.

Just as it is the duty, the privilege, of the strong to help the weak, so it is the duty of the free to help those across this planet who are oppressed because of their beliefs, the colour of their skin, their sex, their poverty, their powerlessness, their principles. We reach out to them, for we must be the friends of those who are oppressed, those who are made captives in their own lands, in our efforts, right throughout this movement, some announced, some more subtle, to secure the release of *refuseniks* and so-called dissidents in the Soviet Union, in our support for *Solidarnosc*, in our aid for the democrats of Chile, in our backing, our solidarity, with the democratically elected government of the Republic of Nicaragua. We stand with them. In all those and in many other ways, in our support for the United Nations, we know that for us as free people freedom can have no boundaries.

Comrades, the Government doesn't know that. Britain should not have to be dragged, fumbling, stumbling and mumbling, into imposing even the most nominal economic sanctions against apartheid South Africa. We should be leading opinion, out of pride in our own liberty and out of the practical knowledge, as we in this movement have counselled for years, that there is only one plausible way that stands the remotest chance of securing peaceful change in South Africa, and that is by the strong imposition of effective economic sanctions against apartheid. Now, when South African businessmen sensibly confer with leaders of the African National Congress, when the United Democratic Front grows bold in its demands for freedom in South Africa and when even the President of the United States of America is obliged to impose embargoes on the apartheid regime, the British government's excuses and alibis become more lame, more pathetic, more contemptible by the day.

Next month is the Commonwealth Heads of Government Conference. Britain will be stranded, isolated amongst that Commonwealth of nations – rich nations, poor nations, black nations, white nations, north and south – as the only nation that shows any degree of friendship towards apartheid South Africa. We should be taking our place in the world properly, with the Australians, the New Zealanders, the Canadians, and the Zambians, the Tanzanians and those who at the front line have made the most monstrous sacrifices in order to sustain what pressure they can on South Africa.

THE NUCLEAR ILLUSIONS

In taking our proper place in the modern world, rid of all the vanities, the nostalgia for a past whose glory missed most of our people, it is essential that we strip ourselves of illusions; most important, that we strip ourselves of the illusions of nuclear grandeur. Not my phrase –

the illusions of nuclear grandeur. That phrase belongs to Field Marshall Lord Carver, former Chief of the Defence Staff. In June he said to the House of Lords:

> *'Why do the Government obstinately persist in wasting money on a so-called British independent deterrent? . . . Our ballistic missiles submarines are not an essential element of NATO's strategy. Whether they are regarded as an addition to the force assigned to the Supreme Allied Commander Europe or as an independent force, they are superfluous and a waste of money. The essential element is the stationing of United States conventional land and air forces on the Continent; and, in order to persuade the American people that it is right, proper and in their own interests that they should continue to [contribute to the defence of Western Europe], it is essential that we and our fellow-European members of NATO should convince them that we are using our money and manpower effectively to maintain . . . the capability of our conventional forces . . . That, my Lords, is the first priority of our defence policy, not illusions of nuclear grandeur.'*

I don't suppose I agree with Field Marshall Lord Carver about everything, but that was a very effective way, from a very effective spokesman, of demonstrating the insanity, the waste, the illusion of Tory Party policy, and demonstrating too the reality and necessity of our complete non-nuclear defence policy to maintain the proper security of our country and alliance. That is our policy, our commitment to the British people, and we will honour it in full.

We want to honour our undertakings in full in every area of policy. We want to say what we mean and mean what we say. We want to keep our promises, and because we want to do that it is essential that we don't make false promises. That is why we must not casually make promises that are so fanciful, so self-indulgent, so exaggerated that they can be completely falsified by the realities in which we live and the realities that we know we shall encounter. If we do not take that view, if we do make false promises, we shall lose integrity, we shall demonstrate immaturity, we will not convince the people.

REALISM, NOT TIMIDITY

Comrades, 463 resolutions have been submitted to this Conference on policy issues, committed honestly, earnestly, and a lot of thought has gone into them. Of those 463, 300 refer to something called the next Labour Government and they refer to what they want that next Labour Government to do. I want to take on many of those commitments. I want to meet many of those demands. I want to respond to many of those calls, in practice – not in words, but in actions. But there is of course a pre-condition to honouring those or any other undertaking that we give. That pre-condition is unavoidable, total and insurmountable. It is the pre-condition that we win a general election. There is absolutely no other way to put any of those policies into effect. The only way to restore, the only way to rebuild, the only way to reinstate, the only way to help the poor, to help the unemployed, to help the victimised, is to get the support of those who are not poor, not unemployed, not victimised, who support our view. That means, comrades, reaching out to them and showing them that we are at one with their decent values and aims, that we are with their hopes for their children, with their needs, with their ideals of justice, improvement and prosperity in the future.

There are some in our movement who, when I say that we must reach out in that fashion, accuse me of an obsession with electoral politics. There are some who, when I say we must reach out and make a broader appeal to those who only have their labour to sell, who are part of the working classes – no doubt about their credentials – say that I am too preoccupied with winning. There are some who say, when I reach out like that and in the course of seeking that objective, that I am prepared to compromise values. I say to them and I say to everybody else, and I mean it from the depths of my soul: there is no need to compromise values, there is no need in this task to surrender our socialism, there is no need to abandon or even try to hide any of our principles. But there is an implacable need to win and there is an equal need for us to understand that we address an electorate which is sceptical, an electorate which needs convincing, a British public who want to know that our idealism is not lunacy, our realism is not timidity, our eagerness is not extremism, a British public who want to know that our carefulness too is not nervousness.

I speak to you, to this Conference. People say that leaders speak to the television cameras. All right, we have got some eavesdroppers. But my belief has always been this, and I act upon it and will always act upon it. I come here to this Conference primarily, above all, to speak to this movement at its Conference. I say to you at this

89

Conference, the best place for me to say anything, that I will tell you what you already know, although some may need reminding. I remind you, every one of you, of something that every single one of you said in the desperate days before June 9, 1983. You said to each other on the streets, you said to each other in the cars rushing round, you said to each other in the committee rooms: elections are not won in weeks, they are won in years. That is what you said to each other. That is what you have got to remember: not in future weeks or future years; this year, this week, this Conference, now – this is where we start winning elections, not waiting until the returning officer is ready.

Secondly, something else you know. If Socialism is to be successful in this country, it must relate to the practical needs and the mental and moral traditions of the men and women of this country. We must emphasise what we have in common with those people who are our neighbours, workmates and fellow countrymen and women – and we have everything in common with them – in a way we could not do if we were remote, if, like the Tories, we were in orbit around the realities of our society, if, like the Social Democrats and the Liberals, we stood off from those realities, retreated from them, deserted them. But we are of, from, for the people. That is our identity, that is our commitment, that is how much we have in common with the people. Let us emphasise that, let us demonstrate it, let us not hide it away as if it was something extraordinary or evidence of reaction. Let us emphasise what we have in common with the people of this country.

We must not dogmatise or browbeat. We have got to reason with people; we have got to persuade people. That is their due. We have voluntarily, every one of us, joined a political party. We wish a lot more people would come and join us, help us, give us their counsel, their energies, their advice, broaden our participation. But in making the choice to join a political party we took a decision, and it was that, by persuasion, we hoped that we could bring more people with us. So that is the basis on which we have got to act, want to act.

Thirdly, something else you know. There is anger in this country at the devastation brought about by these last six years of Tory government, but strangely that anger is mixed with despair, a feeling that the problems are just too great, too complex, to be dealt with by any government or any policy. That feeling is abroad. We disagree with it, we contend it, we try to give people the rational alternatives,

90

but it exists. If our response to that despair, anger and confusion amounts to little more than slogans, if we give the impression to the British people that we believe that we can just make a loud noise and the Tory walls of Jericho will fall down, they are not going to treat us very seriously at all – and we won't deserve to be treated very seriously.

ATTACK ON MILITANT

Fourthly, I shall tell you again what you know. Because you are from the people, because you are of the people, because you live with the same realities as everybody else lives with, implausible promises don't win victories. I'll tell you what happens with impossible promises. You start with far-fetched resolutions. They are then pickled into a rigid dogma, a code, and you go through the years sticking to that, out-dated, misplaced, irrelevant to the real needs, and you end in the grotesque chaos of a Labour council – a *Labour* council – hiring taxis to scuttle round a city handing our redundancy notices to its own workers. I am telling you, no matter how entertaining, how fulfilling to short-term egos – I'm telling you, and you'll listen – you can't play politics with people's jobs and with people's services or with their homes. Comrades, the voice of the people – not the people here; the voice of the real people with real needs – is louder than all the boos that can be assembled. Understand that, please, comrades. In your socialism, in your commitment to those people, understand it. The people will not, cannot, abide posturing. They cannot respect the gesture-generals or the tendency-tacticians.

Comrades, it seems to me lately that some of our number become like latter-day public school-boys. It seems it matters not whether you won or lost, but how you played the game. We cannot take that inspiration from Rudyard Kipling. Those game players get isolated, hammered, blocked off. They might try to blame others – workers, trade unions, some other leadership, the people of the city – for not showing sufficient revolutionary consciousness, always somebody else, and then they claim a rampant victory. Whose victory? Not victory for the people, not victory for them. I see the casualties; we all see the casualties. They are not to be found amongst the leaders and some of the enthusiasts; they are to be found amongst the people whose jobs are destroyed, whose services are crushed, whose living standards are pushed down to deeper depths of insecurity and misery.

THORNS & ROSES

Comrades, these are vile times under this Tory Government for local democracy, and we have got to secure power to restore real local democracy.

But I look around this country and I see Labour councils, I see socialists, as good as any other socialists, who fought the good fight and who, at the point when they thought they might jeopardise people's jobs and people's services, had the intelligence, yes, and the courage to adopt a different course. They truly put jobs and services first before other considerations. They had to make hellish choices. I understand it. You must agonise with them in the choices they had to make – very unpalatable, totally undesirable, but they did it. They found ways. They used all their creativity to find ways that would best protect those whom they employed and those whom they were elected to defend. Those people are leaders prepared to take decisions, to meet obligations, to give service. They know life is real, life is earnest – too real, too earnest to mistake a Conference Resolution for an accomplished fact; too real, to earnest to mistake a slogan for a strategy; too real, too earnest to allow them to mistake their own individual enthusiasms for mass movement; too real, too earnest to mistake barking for biting. I hope that becomes universal too.

Comrades, I offer you this counsel. The victory of socialism, said a great socialist, does not have to be complete to be convincing. I have no time, he went on, for those who appear to threaten the whole of private property but who in practice would threaten nothing; they are purists and therefore barren. Not the words of some hypnotised moderate, not some petrified pragmatist, but Aneurin Bevan in 1950 at the height of his socialist vision and his radical power and conviction. There are some who will say that power and principle are somehow in conflict. Those people who think that power and principle are in conflict only demonstrate the superficiality, the shallowness, of their own socialist convictions; for whilst they are bold enough to preach those convictions in little coteries, they do not have the depth of conviction to subject those convictions, those beliefs, that analysis, to the real test of putting them into operation in power.

CONCLUSION
There is no collision between principle and power. For us as democratic socialists the two must go together, like a rich vein that passes through everything that we believe in, everything that we try to

92

do, everything that we will implement. Principle and power, conviction and accomplishment, going together. We know that power without principle is ruthless and vicious, and hollow and sour. We know that principle without power is naive, idle sterility. That is useless – useless to us, useless to the British people to overcome their travails, useless for our purpose of changing society as democratic socialists. I tell you that now. It is what I have always said, it is what I shall go on saying, because it is what I said to you at the very moment that I was elected leader.

I say to you in complete honesty, because this is the movement that I belong to, that I owe this party everything I have got – not the job, not being leader of the Labour Party, but every life chance that I have had since the time I was a child: the life chance of a comfortable home, with working parents, people who had jobs; the life chance of moving out of a pest and damp-infested set of rooms into a decent home, built by a Labour council under a Labour Government; the life chance of an education that went on for as long as I wanted to take it. Me and millions of others of my generation got all their chances from this movement. That is why I say that this movement, its values, its policies, applied in power, gave me everything that I have got – me and millions like me of my generation and succeeding generations. That is why it is my duty to be honest and that is why it is our function, our mission, our duty – all of us – to see that those life chances exist and are enriched and extended to millions more, who without us will never get the chance of fulfilling themselves. That is why we have got to win, that is what I have always believed and that is what I put to you at the very moment that I was elected.

In 1983 I said to this Conference: 'We have to win. We must not permit any purpose to be superior for the Labour movement to that purpose.' I still believe it. I will go on saying it until we achieve that victory and I shall live with the consequences, which I know, if this movement is with me, will be victory – victory with our policies intact, no sell-outs, provided that we put nothing before the objective of explaining ourselves and reasoning with the people of this country. We will get that victory with our policies, our principles, intact. I know it can be done. Reason tells me it can be done. The people throughout this movement, who I know in huge majority share all these perceptions and visions and want to give all their energies, they know it can be done. Realism tells me it can be done, and the plain realities and needs of our country tell me it must be done. We have got to win, not for our sakes, but really, truly to deliver the British people from evil. Let's do it.

REPLY TO DEBATE ON MINERS' STRIKE

CAN I begin by saying that in this hall and in this movement, in all its unions, throughout the party, there are no donkeys, no jackals, only people. So let us begin by understanding that this is a very basic debate for our movement, one that we have got to resolve not only here but in the course of the next two years and at that general election and beyond, and try to conduct affairs on the basis of the fraternity that everybody ceaselessly is talking about.

The NEC is asking the National Union of Mineworkers to remit this resolution on the grounds that the NEC supports the first part, referring to a review, and supports the second part referring to the reinstatement of victimised miners, and opposes the third part, calling for retrospective reimbursement. So far as that review is concerned, it will in any event take place. It is a normal part of the judicial procedure in this country and, however well grounded our suspicions about the judiciary or about the judicial procedure, that part of it actually does operate. I tell you this: that in pursuit of getting fair treatment for those men in jail, for those going to appeal, for those seeking to get parole, we do them no favour by celebrating the matter of review because there will not be any part of that procedure that will want to give the impression that it has been pressurised, pushed or influenced by an outside political body. That is a fact of life.

Second fact of life. The reinstatement is not something we should just wait until the next Labour Government for. The people who have not been reinstated are, in the overwhelming majority of cases, men who have not only been found guilty of no crime. Most of them have not even been summoned to court or tried for any crime. And yet the NCB has sentenced them to an endless imprisonment in unemployment without parole date, without review. I say this now: that justice demands in any event that the efforts which have already gone into trying to secure reinstatement for the victimised miners, many of them with success, must continue now, and if, by the time we get that Labour Government at the next election, there are still men in the categories that I have described who have committed no crime and do not merit the punishment of continual unemployment, we will bring all pressure and influence to bear to see that that those men are justly restored at proper status to their jobs.

Now what of reimbursement? Arthur said, and others have said, that we have the commitment in this party, that it is a matter of established policy that we have determined the principle. We need some details of that. The principle that Arthur talks about and others talk about was established, I presume, in this Conference in 1982 in very bold, specific, uncompromising terms. The Resolution that was passed said that there would be legislation:

> to provide for reimbursement of any fines levied against trade unionists as a result of Tory legal measures.

The majority could scarcely have been bigger. It was 6.8 million to 66,000. The first thing is, however, that that Resolution was utterly irrelevant to the procedures that have inflicted such damage on the NUM. They have not been done under any Tory laws. They have been done under a common law that provides for an individual to take his union to court. Is anybody seriously suggesting we tear up that common law and the protections for individual assertion? We can disagree profoundly with the people who did it, with their motivations, with the kind of backing they had, yes. But that 6.8 million to 66,000 resolution is redundant so far as this issue is concerned.

Second point. Listen to the facts for once. There was the commitment – 6.8 million to 66,000, well in excess of the two thirds majority which under our constitution requires Clause V meetings of the NEC and the shadow cabinet to consider these matters for inclusion in the manifesto. So it should have been a safe bet for such deliberation. Here is the last election manifesto. Not a word, not a comma, not a jot from that commitment. How did that come about? I tell you, comrades, I was at every one of those joint meetings between the NEC and the Parliamentary Labour Party. I did not hear one single member of that NEC insisting, asking, mentioning that that commitment should be in, not one. That gives us the choice, does it not? Do we warm ourselves at the glow of fine promises in Conference and then just hope, when we come to make manifestos, left, right and centre, trade unionists, parliamentary activists, that somehow the electorate are going to forget in the meantime, just as conveniently as people on the NEC or in the PLP can forget in the meantime, what fine promises in Conference actually came to.

The third fact is this. The precedents have been quoted. The one quoted this morning was that of the 1982 Tory legislation which makes provision for people who have lost their employment as a consequence of failing to become part of a closed shop and providing them with compensation. We fought against that. We fought against the law, we fought against the proposition, we fought against the idea that people should be retrospectively compensated for, frankly, being scabs. I think we were right. But even then, what is the precedent in terms of this resolution? Did anyone say to those people who would not join those closed shops, who wanted to be the freeloaders, 'It's all right, you can risk your job, you can lose your job, because Jim Prior and Norman Tebbit are coming along on white horses.' Did anybody seek to give them reassurances that there would be no consequence to the effect of their action? And were those people in any event, wrong though they were and are, actually contesting the law in the course of their actions? And was a Tory government proposing that they would turn the law upside down for the purposes of associating with and supporting those people? No they were not. The precedent does not stick. Neither do the other precedents. Not Poplar, not the so-called miner's insurrection of 1983. They do not fit. None of those precedents fits because on none of the occasions ever quoted is it the fact that the impression was given by a party in opposition that when it secured power it would offer somehow to give compensation; that when it got to power it could guarantee that actions taken whilst it was in opposition could be undertaken with impunity. It would be utterly dishonest now for this party to give such an undertaking to anybody, individual or institution, that somehow people can come into conflict with the common law, the civil law, the criminal law, and one day, sometime in the future, the cavalry will ride in in the form of a Labour government and pick up the tag. It is not going to happen, and even if we said that it was going to happen, nobody would be convinced in the British public.

Now then, some further facts which are essential to the assessment of this issue. The basic issue, the fundamental issue – Ron Todd, David Basnett and many other people raised it – is helping the miners, supporting the miners. I say to you as the Member of Parliament for a mining constituency that they certainly do need help. In 1983 an overtime ban began. It went on for nineteen weeks. Very few men in the coalfield lost less than one shift a week for those nineteen weeks. Then they went on a twelve-month strike and felt the whole force of a social security system so vicious that it even astonished the opponents of the miners. Then, by the end of the dispute, they and their families were destitute and hugely indebted. During that period – [*in reply to interruption from floor*:] Well, I was not telling them lies. That is what I was not doing during that period. In that period 25,000 jobs were lost in the coalmining industry, an average of 1,400 a month. The conclusion of the strike sees as big a division in the union – which I hope can be healed by the sense of Notts miners voting to stay in the NUM – and, on top of all that, another reason for them wanting, needing and deserving help is that that dispute, that strike, left the management of the National Coal Board with a power, a prerogative, a force that no mining management in Britain has enjoyed for one day since 1947. That is why they need help.

Now, on top of all that, the miners face a terrible dilemma. For, as a consequence of being on strike for that twelve months and not making a sufficient national insurance contribution, if they should become redundant in the calendar year 1986, they are denied unemployment benefit. I find it very strange that at the TUC, in the intervening period and in today's debate, not once has attention been drawn to this potential vast injustice, the awful worry that it inflicts upon the miners, and the fact that it says to coalminers, 'Go and talk to them'. [*interruptions*] Well, that is what they are telling me all the time. They are frightened to death because if they fight now and take the risk of the pit closing in 1986, they face even greater destitution because of the fact that they cannot even claim the dole. That is why the miners need help. On the basis of all those realities they need help, and I find it strange that this latest crisis for those families has not even been mentioned.

They are in the state where young men are accepting redundancy to pay off the debts that they ran up during the strike. It is pathetic, terrible, to see what they have been driven to. And all the time the question is asked: 'How did it come to that?' I will give you the answer of a lodge official in my constituency, a man who was on strike from the first day to the last, who picketed continuously, whose wife and family backed him to the hilt. He said to me: 'We knew about the Ridley plan. We knew we had a government of particular ruthlessness. We knew there was a build-up of coal stocks. We knew that the refusal to strike had been registered in successive ballots. We knew that the overtime ban had lost us shifts. We knew then that of all the times to call a coalmining strike, the end of the winter is just about the point in the calendar least appropriate.' They are his words. 'The fact,' he said, 'that it was called without a ballot denied to the miners unity and it denied to the miners the solidarity of so much of the rest of the trade union movement. On top of all that,' he said, 'we were given continued, repeated promises that coal stocks were at the point of exhaustion, and it never was true. They were never at the point of exhaustion.'

The strike wore on. The violence built up because the single tactic chosen was that of mass picketing, and so we saw policing on a scale and with a system that has never been seen in Britain before. The court actions came, and by the attitude to the court actions, the NUM leadership ensured that they would face crippling damages as a consequence. To the question: 'How did this position arise?', the man from the lodge in my constituency said: 'It arose because nobody really thought it out.'

Now in those circumstances we ask how do we help miners. How do we help them? By one means. By getting a Labour government that is committed to giving proper priority to the coalmining industry, investment in coal, use of coal, and if pits close through exhaustion alternatives to employment in coal; a Labour government that would replace the current leadership of the National Coal Board. That is the way to help the miners. It is a fact that if we were ever to endorse the idea of retrospective reimbursement we would harm our chances because people would be very confused about our attitude towards the rule of law and we would give heavy calibre ammunition to our enemies to misrepresent us, to defame us and to demolish the hope that the miners have got of getting support from a Labour government.

But don't let the electoral consideration dictate your actions at all. Don't let a political party take any notice of electoral considerations. That would be class treachery, wouldn't it? Decide it on the basis of right and wrong. The wrong of it is that we would be making an entirely false promise to those who endure continual suffering and we would be giving the impression that we were prepared to extend a form of immunity regardless of the circumstances, and that we could never do. We know what the state does, what the judicial system is. Do you think you can make it better by copying the tactics of the Tories? Do you think you can make it better by having the same corrupt attitude towards the law of this land? That is not our Labour movement. That is not democratic socialism.

I say this in closing. Let us now go to the vote. I ask one thing in that vote, just one thing. That is that as you vote be sure that you can convincingly justify the way that you vote, not here in the tight circles, the comfortable, warm circles of the Labour Party Conference, but in the street, to your neighbours, at work, wherever you go, in interviews. Justify it there. I could not justify it. That is why in honesty I say, if the NUM does not remit, please oppose the resolution so that we really can help the miners, the men who cut the coal.

1986
BLACKPOOL

'I would never let
my country die for me'

Labour's 1986 conference was calmer than the previous year's. The process of expelling Liverpool's leading Militants, including Hatton, had got under way during the summer; arguments about the miners' strike had begun to lose their passion; Labour had edged ahead of both the Alliance and the Conservatives in the opinion polls. All in all, delegates arrived at Blackpool in far higher spirits than they had descended on Bournemouth twelve months before.

The 1986 conference also looked different. It was the first to bear the imprint of Peter Mandelson, Labour's new director of communications. The platform was given a more modern design. Bright red was discarded in favour of cream-and-pink. The red flag was dropped as Labour's symbol and replaced by the rose (the most common symbol for other western European socialist parties). When Kinnock spoke, he appeared on television against a plain background, uncluttered by other members of the platform party. Mandelson's exercise was designed to demonstrate two things – that Labour had modernised itself, and that the purpose of the annual conference was to impress voters watching on television as much as delegates in the hall.

Of the more substantive issues debated at Blackpool, the most important was defence. A few days earlier the Liberal Assembly at Eastbourne had voted narrowly to reject an agreement between David Steel and David Owen that Britain should retain nuclear weapons, if necessary by co-operating with France to create a 'Eurobomb'. The Eastbourne vote had caused disarray within the Liberal/SDP Alliance, and seemed to give Labour, for once, the opportunity to appear united on defence.

Labour's hopes were short-lived. The BBC's Panorama had planned a report on Labour's defence policy, to be broadcast on the

Monday evening of the party's conference. Advance publicity for the programme announced that Caspar Weinberger, the United States' Defence Secretary, would criticise Labour's plans to close US nuclear bases in Britain. He warned that if a Kinnock government took this step, America might retaliate by closing all its bases in Britain.

In Blackpool, Kinnock was asked to react to Weinberger's intervention – and to the even more brutal comment by Weinberger's colleague, assistant defence secretary Richard Perle, that Labour's policy was 'wildly irresponsible'. Kinnock was angry that Weinberger and Perle had departed from the convention that government officials refrain from public comments about the internal party arguments of friendly nations. Kinnock told reporters: 'Another country cannot interfere with the life of a democratically elected government.'

Kinnock was embarrassed further by Panorama's interview with Denis Healey, Labour's shadow foreign secretary. Healey was asked whether America might dissuade an incoming Labour government from insisting on a withdrawal of US nuclear bases. Healey's answer seemed to open the door to precisely such a change: 'I don't think the Americans could persuade us, but I think if we take the alliance seriously we have to listen to what our allies feel as a whole.'

Pressed further to say whether Labour might change its policy if other NATO countries wanted it to do so, Healey said: 'I would doubt it but it's not inconceivable.' Journalists and left-wingers seized on the phrase 'it's not inconceivable'. Did it signal the leadership's intention to ditch a vital element of its non-nuclear policy?

The next day, in his conference speech, Kinnock made no direct reference to Weinberger, Perle or Healey. He did, however, insist that his passion for unilateralism remained undimmed: 'I would fight and die for my country, but I tell you I would never let my country die for me.' At the same time, Kinnock went out of his way to praise the American administration's 'common sense' – implying that Weinberger and Perle had not been speaking for President Reagan. Kinnock also attempted to assure the Americans that he would allow their intelligence-gathering and early warning operations to continue unhindered. The defence section of Kinnock's speech went some way to limiting the damages of the previous forty-eight hours, but did nothing to end his continuing discomfiture over Labour's nuclear policy.

PK

WE ARE meeting in the autumn of this eighth year of Thatcherism – ninety months of Maggie, ninety months in which our society has become more divided than at any time since the Second World War, ninety months in which our industry has been devastated as never before, in which our economy has been weakened as never before; and still, after all that, the Prime Minister says that she seeks another term. Well, she is not going to have another term. We and the British people together will definitely see to that. And not all of the creative genius of Mr Jeffrey Archer or the sweetness and sourness of Mrs Edwina Currie can change that course of events. Not even the Chairman of the Conservative Party, Norman Tebbit, Mr Punch set to control all the puppets, can change that course of history, for all his scare tactics, which are such proof of a scared party that he chairs.

We have had those years of Thatcherism and we are also, of course, in the sixth year of the coagulation of the Liberals and the Social Democratic Party. At last David Steel and David Owen are finding out that it takes more than fishing trips and Edinburgh Festival visits and French leave to make either a policy or a party. And if they did not know before, they certainly know now, after a Liberal gathering last week which will long be remembered as the Assembly which put the lie in Alliance.

It should not really have come as such a surprise that they voted as they did on defence, on civil nuclear power and on many other things. They did after all have the inspirational experience of being addressed by Dr Owen at their very first session of the Assembly. To be fair to Dr Owen, he is unique. He wanted to dominate the Labour Party. He failed in that. He is trying to dominate the Liberal Party. He is going to fail in that too. They do tell me that some Conservatives fancy an association with Dr Owen. I think he ought to carry a political health

105

warning to political parties. In any case, the Conservatives should be cautious. After Mrs Thatcher, once bitten, twice shy.

As the Tories fade and as the Liberals and Social Democrats falter, this party – our party – is entering its fourth year of recovery and of advance. That recovery has been worked for by people right across the movement, in every part of the movement. In the local authorities where people have had to endure the most crushing pressures and have still fought their way through, in the trade union movement, which has been subject to incessant attacks from every quarter, from unemployment, from the courts, from the prejudice-made statute that is so much part of the Tory codes against free trade unionism in this country. It has been fought for and worked for too by rank-and-file members right through this party, who have worked as never before to get our message of jobs and justice to the British people with an effectiveness that we have never shown before.

We have been making that recovery through a unity of purpose without which all else would have been absolutely impossible. We have been making that recovery by listening to people, by heeding people, and not straggling behind the lowest pace of opinion, but never wandering away from the main trail either, so far as to lose sight of the main thread of public opinion. We have made the recovery also, in this democratic socialist party, by ensuring that we sustain both our democracy and our socialism. We have not done it in an authoritarian manner. We have done it because we could not allow our democracy to be distorted, we could not allow our generosity to be abused in this democratic socialist party. We have done it by natural justice to them and, yes, we have done justice to ourselves. In all of that, we have earned new strength by hard work, by effort.

Of course there is more to do. There always is more to do. First, there is no feeling of satisfaction, no threshold of support on which we will rest contented. It is a fond presumption among a few pundits that we hide ourselves away and do fancy arithmetic to find out what neat arrangement of Tory and Liberal and Social Democratic support will give us the highest number of seats with the lowest number of votes. Well, I can tell them we don't do that. We are not in that dangerous game; in fact we are not in a game at all. We are in the serious and sustained task of convincing more people, of putting our ideas and our policies and of persuading people to our view. That is the way in which we search for power, not by some roll of the dice, but on the basis of the effort that we are prepared to make to gain the mandate in this democracy. We will go on doing that and we will go on gaining and keeping support from everyone who is prepared to hear our message, everyone who is prepared to give us the democratic chance to show just what we can do.

We have seen of course what others do. We have seen their seven savage years; we have seen what they have done to our country. Given declining unemployment in 1979, they have increased it by over two million. Given restored manufacturing investment in 1979, they have cut investment and destroyed capacity so that manufacturing investment is still 20 per cent below the level that it was when they took over. Given a working body of manufacturing industry in 1979, they have lopped off whole limbs of manufacturing industry. Given a stable world trade position in 1979, they have lost 22 per cent of our share of world trade. Given the fantastic bonus of £50,000 million of oil revenues, they have blown it – wasted it – on the massive bills caused by the unemployment which their policies have generated. That and much more – so much more – makes them a government unfit to govern. They are rulers who, in Percy Shelley's words: 'Neither see nor feel nor know, but leechlike to their fainting country cling'. Leechlike they have increased interest rates and the tax burdens; leechlike they have allowed the drain-off of investment capital from this investment-hungry country.

Those rulers, who neither see nor feel nor know, have cut house-building, training, research and development, the Health Service, education. And these are not just attacks on institutions; these are direct attacks on individuals and their liberties, families and their needs. That is what those rules have been doing in their blindness, their stupidity, their malice, in the past seven years. And all the time they have been doing that we have heard these strident homilies about Victorian values and about morality. Homilies on the virtues on self-reliance, when millions would like nothing more than to have the rudimentary means to be self-reliant. Homilies on the virtues of thrift, when families in poverty are constantly humiliated as they try to clothe and feed themselves and their children. Homilies on the virtues of responsibility, when the rights of those who care for old and sick and disabled loved ones are secured only by the interventions of the European Court, and even then what is given with one hand by the judgement of the court is taken away with the other by a government that denies resources to the carers of this country.

Mrs. Thatcher says that her policies start with the freedom and well-being of the family. When there are six million people in this country now so impoverished that they cannot even afford essential items of clothing, when there are two million children living in families dependent on supplementary benefit, when one in four families in Britain is living in sub-standard housing, when thousands of homeless families are condemned to the appalling conditions of bed and breakfast accommodation, the Prime Minister lectures the family, lectures the country, on morality.

She has a sort of clone now as Under-Secretary of State for the Health Service, who recommended but last week that a high-fibre diet should replace the National Health Service. It reminded me of the Tory lady who in the depression was generous enough to give lectures to the families of the unemployed on what nourishing soup they could make with fish-heads, until one woman in the front said: 'That's very nice, my lady, but could you tell us who has the rest of the fish.'

We get the lectures on morality when the Silentnight Company, when British Coal, when News International desert their basic obligations to those people who have given them faithful years of service. It is the people outside who are lectured on morality and never those who sit in the offices inside. I suppose that the pious sermons and self-righteous homilies from Mrs Thatcher and Mr Tebbit are easier than facing the real problems or answering the real questions, and there are plenty of those, plenty of those real moral questions. When it is so obvious that a drugs plague endangers young people in our country, why get rid of one in nine customs officers, why sack 900 customs officers, whose job it is to restrain the importation of drugs?

Another question: when it is so obvious that dark streets and labyrinthine housing estates and insecure doors and windows give such freedom to criminals and such terror to people, especially old people, why not invest in repairs and in strengthening and lighting those streets, so that people can enjoy real security and the criminals can be defeated? When violence is such a terrible menace, especially violence against women, why can't the laws against beating the abuse that already exist be fully and rigorously enacted and enforced in this country? Why can't that be the case, so that we can free victims from the perpetual fear of the returning brutal husband, so that the guilty can be punished or treated for whatever sickness it is makes a man hit a woman? We will see that those laws are enforced. We will make the investment in security. We will see that the customs officers are there as part of the partnership against the drug menace.

There are other areas too where there are moral questions. When it is clear that thousands of lives could be saved and terrible anxiety and pain relieved by an effective system of cervical cancer screening, by an increase in the treatment of kidney ailments, by the maintenance of medical research, why close down the cervical and breast cancer screening facilities? Why make cuts which prevent dialysis and treatment? Why impose reductions that terminate research programmes and send some of our best young scientists abroad to work in other countries, away from our land, when it is obvious that death rates, mental and physical sickness rates, suicide and family breakdown rates are all much higher amongst the unemployed than they are amongst the employed? Why not fight unemployment as we will instead of simply saying that it is disappointing or one of the two great mysteries of our time, as Mrs Thatcher does?

These people, these Tories, dress up the get-rich-quick society as the opportunity society. They continually represent arrogance and aggression as the only truth of strength. They have dedicated every policy to making the very rich richer and the poor poorer. They flaunt the commercial paradise before the young people of this country, but with unemployment and insecurity at a mass level among the young of this country they inflict a purgatory on the young who have been promised so much. With their 40p pensions rise and their cuts in concessionary fares, community care and housing and benefits they daily – these moralists – preach the commandment that teaches us 'Honour thy father and thy mother'. That is the morality of this government.

BRITAIN'S MORAL MAJORITY
I look at all that and I ask myself: 'Just where do they get their idea of morality?', and the British people ask the same question. There is a great grouping in our society which opposes the malice and the meanness of Toryism. There is a huge number which abominates the dual standards and the double-talk sermons. There is in this country – there always has been; there always will be – a moral majority. It is not

a narrow, bigoted, self-righteous grouping; it is a broadminded and compassionate grouping of people. That majority is not sentimental, for it knows that sentiment is very cheap. That majority is realistic too, for it knows that if its morality is to have practical effect it must be backed by the material provision provided in justice.

We as democratic socialists make our appeal to that moral majority. It does not expect politicians to deliver heaven on earth. It does expect politicians to work to stop hell on earth. That is what the moral majority demands in this country. A part of that majority would consider themselves well blessed if they had just a roof over their head, if they had a job to go to, if they knew that the colour of their skin inflicted no extra disadvantage on them. They would feel well blessed if they did not have to fear electricity or gas bills with all the tortuous anxiety of poverty. If they could afford a pair of shoes for the children without being fearful of an economic crisis in the family, they would consider themselves to be well blessed.

Of course, there are millions who do not live in that condition of penury and many of those – I meet them – are not themselves impoverished or insecure. But they still say to me: 'We are not badly off, but we can't get our Mam into hospital', 'We are not badly off, but with two younger children at home we just haven't got the room to accept the daughter and the son-in-law. They can't come and live with us', 'We are not badly off, I am working, my husband is working, but our twenty-year-old has never had a job and our sixteen-year-old is leaving school this year and doesn't know where to start looking for a job' – people in security themselves but surrounded by all the evidence and all the pressures of insecurity which comes over their own doorsteps.

There are millions too who are not even affected at that range by the problems, but who consider that we need a government which will try to use policies which begin to attend to those material needs and fulfill those moral obligations. They want a government which does not preach the pious sermons of Maggie's morality but practises the policies of provision. They want a government which will back up its morality by policies, by determined effort to operate policies of investment, of production, of growth, of employment. We, indeed only we, will provide that government for Britain, and in doing that we will be guided by four basic facts of our condition.

•   First, there is no prospect of a sustainable reduction in unemployment in this country unless we can attain stable, long-term growth

- Secondly, there is no possibility of long-term growth and resilient prosperity for the British economy without a major development of British manufacturing industry.
- Thirdly, the length of our relative economic decline and the way in which it has deteriorated and has been accelerated and intensified in the last seven years presents our country with a new set of strategic problems to which there must be a new set of strategic answers.
- Fourthly, none of the major social, commercial, industrial or employment problems that we face is self-correcting. The market will not look after those problems; it can only worsen those problems. If they are to be overcome, systematic planned action must be taken by government, and it must be taken in concert with all the participants in the economy, to construct the framework of the educational, economic, technical and social conditions within which this economy can thrive again.

LABOUR'S INDUSTRY POLICY

We have to operate on a new agenda and we need new instruments, new policies, for that strategic change. We have to combat slump now and simultaneously foster the structure of change necessary to stop and to reverse the long-term deficiencies and decline which pre-date even Mrs. Thatcher's rule. On that new agenda is our new two-year programme to combat unemployment and bring unemployment down by one million, by generating jobs that need to be done for people who need to do them in a country which needs them to be done – jobs in construction, jobs in cleansing our environment, jobs in training people, caring for people. And on the new agenda too there is our five-year, medium-term employment strategy, which has the objective of laying the foundation of steadily expanding investment and employment. And then, at the same time, the implementation of a ten-year planning horizon which is essential to provide the continuity of development, which takes proper account of the change in the pace and the scale of technology, of trade, of employment, so that we are not caught without warning or overwhelmed with our change in the way successive generations have been.

For all those reasons it is essential that investment finance is

111

returned to this country and retained in this country. That is why we shall introduce our capital repatriation scheme. If we were to leave it just at that, it is possible that the money would be in Britain but would not be used for the maximum benefit of our country in any coherent fashion at all. Other countries, indeed our most successful competitor countries, have institutions which provide the necessary coherence in allocating funds for investment and growth, and we need such an institution too. That is why we are establishing the British Investment Bank, to give investors the dual advantage of investing in Britain and getting a rate of return that compares with what they could get elsewhere. Some of those funds will be taken up by companies large and small which have in existence worthwhile and specific investment ideas.

In other cases we need finance to restructure and to modernise, to create and to nurture new industries. It is for that reason that we will be establishing British Enterprise as a holding company engaged in putting social ownership into practice through taking shares or complete proprietorship of enterprises which are critical to growth and investment in our country. That system of social ownership embraces activity from small co-operatives to municipal enterprises and right through to the majority utility corporations like British Telecom which, in the strategic interests of this country, must come back into full social ownership.

The purpose of a practical programme is to produce our way to sustainable recovery, to sponsor new technologies, to strengthen consistent research and development, to promote our export trade and to provide employment. Comrades, I have said it before, I will say it again and again and again: we must literally make our way to recovery, produce our way to recovery, sell our way to recovery in the world. For there is no other way we can fully earn the living that we want for ourselves and for our children. That has got to be understood, and there are some other factors that have got to be understood too.

If we invest in production and provision, and we will, and if we restore and extend social and personal services, and we will, and if we pay better pensions and help the poor and the disabled, and we are going to, then what we have got to make sure of is that the extra demand that we sponsor does not all go on the purchase of foreign finished goods. For if it were the case, that it was actually making jobs

112

not in Britain but in Japan and in Germany, then the effort will have been kindly but it won't have been very constructive. It would be stimulating, but the result would not be very substantial. Secondly, and equally crucial, if those different policies of growth under a different government of growth were to bring rises in capital costs or in labour costs beyond what could be absorbed by efficiency, beyond what could be tolerated by purchasers, then the chance of significant development and increasing employment would be wiped away.

There is in this country now a great reservoir of injustice and impatience, which has been built up and is still building in these years of Thatcherism. I know that. You know that. We can empty those reservoirs of injustice by deliberate and persistent policies and by sticking to our strategy, but if we tried to do it in any other way than by persistence, by being systematic and by sticking to our strategy, if we simply tried to open the floodgates, then the prospect of renewal and recovery would be washed out.

That is why we are not going to do that. We cannot. We will not. And our decisions about those things will not be governed by obedience to convention or to some fancy idea of political virility. Those decisions are governed by reality, guided constantly by the determination to generate jobs, to rebuild industry, to re-establish justice in our country. And those decisions, those policies, will operate best and most fruitfully in partnership with trade unionists and with managers who understand that if we were to try to do everything at once we would end by doing nothing at all. That is why our priority for jobs, for growth and for fighting poverty must be strict and straight, and it must be sustained. That is how it will be. Whilst the speed may vary, because it would be ridiculous to assume that somehow we inoculated ourselves against the realities of the movement and the marketing which we must sell to the world, the direction of those policies, of those decisions, will unerringly and unreservedly be towards economic recovery and structural change all the time.

That is the reason for establishing our new instruments of the British Investment Bank and British Enterprise. That is the reason for our approach to social ownership. We need to ensure that the right money is in the right places, available to people who want to make, to invest and to employ. Like any family or any business or any country we are going to have to raise money in order to invest in the means of making wealth. Some of the money will come as we cut unemployment, some of the money will come through the repatriation scheme and some of it we shall borrow, and what we have to borrow is about an extra 2 per cent of the total income of this country.

Despite the fact that she is the greatest borrower in British history, Mrs Thatcher is constantly saying that she won't do that, she won't borrow. She won't increase borrowing by that extra 2 per cent of national income in order to fund development. She says she won't do that because she is not prepared to leave the burden of debt to our children. That is very touching. Or at least it would be touching if it wasn't so cruelly obvious that Mrs Thatcher is prepared to leave our children with a legacy of decay and decline right through our society. Somehow she doesn't care that the result of not spending is increasing unemployment now and a guarantee of future unemployment, future under-employment, future under-investment, yes, future under-development in our country. It is one thing to say to your children, since she is so concerned about the children: 'I leave you with the house and the remainder of the mortgage to pay after my day'. That is the prudent way, that is the careful way. It is another thing altogether to say to your children: 'Because I wouldn't pay the mortgage. I will leave you nowhere to live after my days.' That is the Thatcher option. That is the imprudent, careless way.

A SOCIALIST FOREIGN POLICY

We Socialists, conscious of the fact that we cannot and do not serve just one generation, conscious that each generation depends upon another, that one generation inherits in the very course of its preparation for the next generation, that there is this continual thread of dependence between the generations of human beings, we Socialists always try to leave this place a little better than when we found it, and that attitude is not confined just to our own country. It is a definition of our view of the world. It is a perception which is more necessary now than it has ever been, for in our one world the dangers know no boundaries. Famine spreads like a contagion. The poisons of pollution spread with the winds and the tides and become more noxious, more dangerous all the time. Terrorism and warfare impose the rule of fear upon millions of people across this globe. People of so many countries face the crises of insecurity, inequality, injustice and exploitation. Throughout our world aggression and oppression and starvation kill peace, and they kill people and they kill hope and they kill freedom.

Afghanistan is still occupied by an invading empire, Iran and Iraq are still engaged in a merciless war of fanaticism. In Chile, Pinochet tramples into his fourteenth year of dictatorship and the people of Nicaragua are struggling to keep their infant democracy alive against the attacks of terrorists armed and funded by the government of the United States of America. Those people of Nicaragua must look at pictures of the 4th of July celebrations and wonder what it can be that makes the United States of America, the great democracy, itself born in revolution, finance evil people to murder the innocent of Nicaragua. What makes them do that? They must ask themselves, as we ask: 'How can a President who is so rightly the enemy of terrorism, as any sane person is, sponsor the terrorism of the Contras in Central America.'

In friendship and in frankness we say to the United States: 'It is wrong to arm the Contra forces. It is wrong to try and squeeze the life out of that poor country of Nicaragua. It is wrong even in your own terms in the USA'. For it is clear that if Nicaragua ever went into any form of partnership with the Soviet Union, it will have been pushed there by poverty and not pulled there by desire. If Nicaragua did become a Russian outpost, the reason would lie in the White House and not in the Kremlin. That is why we say in friendship and in frankness to our fellow democracy in the USA: 'Treating near-by nations as neighbours is one thing; treating those countries as if they were bits of your backyard is another thing altogether.' Long ago in the United States of America and elsewhere the human race decided that it was wrong for one person to try to own another person. Long ago in a revolutionary war in 1776 they decided in America and elsewhere that it was wrong for one country to try to own another country, and what was right in America and between America and Britain in 1776 and what was right about our view of Russia and the Eastern European countries in 1946 is surely right about the USA and Nicaragua in 1986.

Just as it is wrong for one country to seek to impose its ownership on another, so it is wrong for one race to impose its domination on another. That is why apartheid is so wrong. That is why apartheid must be ended. Apartheid truly is a crime against humanity. And while it remains, none of the people of South and Southern Africa will be truly free, no one in the white minority will know real security, no one in the black majority will know anything resembling real liberty, no one in the neighbouring countries will be able to live in real security. That is why we want to hasten the day of change to a democratic South Africa, and the lever which we have long ago chosen for that purpose is strict and strong sanctions against South Africa. They are the only practical means of trying to promote an end to apartheid that is not soaked in the blood of millions.

Such sanctions are of course resisted by some. Mrs Thatcher, Herr Kohl, President Reagan refuse to promote a regime of robust sanctions. The excuse that they offer for refusing to impose the implacable pressures that are necessary against apartheid is that such pressure, such sanctions would be immoral because they would inflict upon the poor further wounds of suffering and destitution. I hear the President, I hear the Prime Minister, I hear the Chancellor and I hear different voices too. I hear louder voices. I hear voices of greater authenticity and greater authority upon the business of the future of the people of South Africa. It is the voice that comes straight from that bitter and bleeding land of South Africa and it does not come from the high-faluting politicians or people in hotels or air-conditioned suites. That voice I hear from South Africa comes from the townships and it comes from the homelands and it comes from the Churches and it comes from the trade unions. It comes from Nelson Mandela in prison, it comes from Archbishop Tutu in his palace. It is the voice that says, in the words of Chief Albert Uthuli: 'Shorten the day of bloodshed, impose those sanctions, aid us in our efforts to end apartheid and oppression.'

This is the Labour Party. We will form the Labour Government. We will answer that call for sanctions from the people of South Africa. We will impose those strict and stringent and comprehensive sanctions. And with the people of South Africa we shall overcome. We shall overcome apartheid with those people and we shall overcome the instability and the terror of Southern Africa as we go about that. We shall take common action in common cause for common good. That is necessary in so many areas, and that fact is now more obvious to more people than ever before.

In this year of 1986, a prophet of that fact, who gave us much more than his prophecies, was killed in his own capital city, out for an evening with his wife. This year we lost my dear comrade and a friend of the world, Olav Palme, a man who gave his intellect to the best possible employment, which is providing practical solutions to the practical problems of humanity. Olav was killed, and the memorial that we have to erect to him is to demonstrate that his instruction about the community of interest across the boundaries of the world has not been lost on this generation and that we work for his objectives in his memory. It is necessary more than ever before.

Within two weeks of April of this year two events, thousands of miles apart, originating from entirely different sources, came together to form an equation in the minds of millions of people in this country and throughout the rest of the world. The bombing of Tripoli and the explosion at Chernobyl demonstrated in the starkest possible way the fragility of our world, the interdependence of its countries and peoples; the need to understand new realities and to provide new responses for our survival depends upon it ultimately. Those responses include the question of the defence of our country and our system of values.

THE CASE FOR NON-NUCLEAR DEFENCE

I hold it to be self-evident that it is the first duty of any government to ensure the security of the country over which it governs, especially if that government is elected by democracy. That duty does not change in any age, and we will discharge that duty fully, for this is our country and we defend our country, as we always have. Meeting that obligation requires that we defend ourselves effectively by land, sea and air and that we participate properly in the Alliance of which we are full and firm members. We will fulfil that obligation, and that is amongst the most prominent of reasons for implementing a non-nuclear defence strategy. For it is now plainly the case that, by pursuing a nuclear-dependent defence policy, the present government is diminishing the conventional defence of our country.

The Ministry of Defence documents – the so-called towpath papers, which were published three weeks ago – give the consequences of the Trident programme as being just for the Navy – not for any of the other services, just for the Navy: major reductions in our conventionally armed submarine fleet, a 20 per cent stretch in the lifetime of our service fleet and a new wave of privatisation in the defence sector like the indefensible and dangerous sell-off of the royal dockyard in Devonport, with all the job losses that that will involve. Not only does that mean that the government is failing to meet the defence needs of Britain. It also means that, because of that increased dependence on nuclear weapons, because of that diminished dependence on conventional arms, the nuclear threshold is lowered. There is no enhanced security for our country in that. There is only increased jeopardy for our country.

That is why we say that at this time of choice the alternatives before the British people are very clear. One alternative is a Tory policy which, in the very act of building up nuclear armaments at ruinous cost, erodes conventional defence and adds to nuclear danger without enhancing in any way national security for Britain. The other alternative is our policy, a policy which responds to the realities, ends the nuclear illusions and properly meets the conventional defence needs and duties of our country. They are the real alternatives, although until a short time ago Dr Owen, Mr Steel and parts of the press would have sought to persuade us that there was a third alternative – the so-called Euro-bomb.

Apart from the fact that it is overwhelmingly rejected as an option by the British people, it is an option without substance, the product of a weekend break in Paris, which had as its function a patching up of a widening crack in the defence positions of the SDP and the Liberal Party. If it ever was in any way feasible, it would mean fingers on the nuclear trigger and a great hole torn in the whole idea and treaty arrangements of non-proliferation. It would mean highest jeopardy at lowest security at maximum cost. It would not influence friends, it would not impress potential enemies, it would not buy us a seat at any disarmament conference or give us essential control over the life and death decisions that effect our country. They call it the Euro-bomb. They call it the minimum deterrent, when it could kill sixty or seventy million people. They can call it those names as long as they like, but in reality it would not be increased security; it would be the *entente terminale*. It has nothing to do with protecting our country or our continent and everything to do with the attempt of the Liberal and SDP leaders to conjure an illusion of a policy out of a delusion of grandeur. No wonder they were rejected.

Of course in recent days there have been some other intervening voices from outside Britain. Some of the language has been lurid, but it has been repudiated. It has been made clear that it is not the representative voice of the attitude of the administration – at least, not representative of the American administration but representative perhaps of the current British administration. The reports are of the

Tories asking for a particular element in the United States of America to help combat our defence policies in this democracy. The conclusion is plain. The interventions that we have heard in recent weeks are not so much the product of American anxiety as a result of Tory alarm at the fact that we are defeating them and we are going to beat them in the next general election. And they will pull any dirty tricks they can in order to try and prevent that.

The attitude of the American administration shows a great deal more common sense and common interest than the Tory attitude. It arises from the knowledge that if a member of the Alliance of these democracies were to seek to subordinate the policies of a democratically elected allied government, it would be invalidating the very principles of democracy and sovereignty which NATO exists to defend and always has existed to defend.

There is another reason for that common sense and common interest. It is that here in Britain and in our territories elsewhere across the world, there are installations which are critical to the defence and intelligence needs of the United States of America, from the early warning system at Fylingdales to the submarine-watching system in Pembrokeshire; from GCHQ to Cyprus; from Hong Kong to Edzell in Scotland. They are essential facilities for the national interests of the United States and the collective interests of the NATO Alliance. We do not propose for one moment, and we never have proposed for one moment, that those facilities should be withdrawn from the Americans, for they are our allies and we honour the Alliance. But it does demonstrate that we play and will continue to play our part in providing security for the American people, and no United States government will sacrifice that essential link in their security.

In all of these matters modern men and modern women, whatever their office, whatever their status, whatever their country, whatever their politics or lack of politics, face the fact that the terrible existence of nuclear weapons puts us in a condition unknown to any previous generation of humankind. We are the first generation in history to have to deal with those weapons, the first generation in history to have to deal not just with the weapons of horror which inflict such dreadful death and suffering during wars but with the existence of weapons of total obliteration. That gives us different challenges and requires different responses. The knowledge must not make people panic;

hysteria is not the response. But it must mean that people face that fact of the existence of weapons of obliteration and how we control, reduce and abolish then squarely and honestly.

I face those questions as the leader of this party who works to become the democratically elected leader of this country. I face those facts too as an adult, as a citizen and as a father. I tell you in no casual spirit, no bravado, that like most of my fellow citizens I would if necessary fight and die, fight and lay down my life for my country and what it stands for. I would fight and die for my country, but I tell you I would never let my country die for me.

CONCLUSION

In everything we do in this party in every part of it we refuse to submit to the idea that the present and future are beyond control. We will not bow down to the defeatism that says that our economy is so badly wounded that it is incapable of renewal. We will not succumb to the defeatism that says that the tensions and dangers and the poisons of the world are so great as to make conflict and contamination inevitable. We look at the weaknesses of our country and we look at the menaces to humankind and we say that inasmuch as these conflicts and dangers are made by human hand, so they can be unmade by human hand. Just as these horrors are made by human error, so they can be unmade by human effort.

That is not a blind attitude. It is not lightly put. It is not evidence of innocence. On the contrary, it is the starkest reality of all. For we either surrender to hopelessness or we stand and fight against it. For us as democratic socialists there is no real choice. We stand and we fight against hopelessness. It is fundamental to our socialism. It is essential to the case that we put to the people of this country, and it is our country: we have nowhere else to go and we have nowhere else that we want to go. That is the investment that we make in it. This is our living space. It is the living space that we want to leave secure, prosperous, just and free to our children. That is the reason why we ask the people of this country to give us democratic power, and it is because we ask for those reasons that they will elect us to that democratic power.

1987
BRIGHTON

'There is no collision between
affluence and socialism'

Labour's 1987 conference took place in the sobering aftermath of the party's crushing general election defeat. Far from toppling Mrs Thatcher, the party had gained only twenty seats compared with 1983; it remained 146 seats short of the Tories – and ninety-seven away from a Commons majority. Kinnock had enjoyed high personal ratings during the campaign, but nothing could disguise the unpopularity of Labour's policies. It was distrusted on the economy, taxation, the trade unions and defence. And despite Kinnock's onslaught on Militant, Labour continued to be thought by many voters to be under the spell of the 'loony left', especially in London.

The most important proposal on the conference agenda was that the party should launch a policy review. This was the brainchild of Tom Sawyer, the deputy general secretary of the National Union of Public Employees and chairman of Labour's Home Policy Committee. Sawyer believed that Labour needed to rethink all aspects of its political strategy. One way to do this would be for the leadership simply to announce new policies and bully the membership into line. Sawyer did not believe this would work. He thought that better and more acceptable policies would emerge from a lengthy period of open debate and widespread consultation. When left-wingers accused Sawyer of planning to abandon Labour's principles, he retorted that for his critics, 'the only true test of radicalism is a deep conservatism in thought and ideas'.

In different senses, both Sawyer and his critics were right. Labour's existing policies rendered the party unelectable. They needed to be rethought if the party was ever to win power. On the other hand, the inevitable terminus of this process would be the death of some of the Left's most cherished projects – on defence, Europe, public spending and public ownership. The only real doubt concerned how long it

123

would take Labour to reach that destination, and what tribulations it would suffer along the way.

Kinnock's wisest course might have been to contract severe laryngitis and say nothing to the 1987 conference. Were he to defend existing policies he could be mocked when they changed; were he to outline his ideas for new policies he would have been accused of pre-empting the process of review. His speech, therefore, was notable for its dearth of policy content. Commentators who looked (as I did) for a candid confession of past errors were disappointed. That summer Mikhail Gorbachev had regaled the Soviet Communist Party Conference with a catalogue of its failings, and was widely praised for his frankness. Kinnock declined to follow his example.

Instead, he sought to separate those on Labour's Left that he hoped could be won to fresh thinking from those he regarded as beyond redemption. He attacked those 'who "have do not disturb" notices hung on their minds', and quoted Aneurin Bevan on the dangers of holding on to 'old words . . . when the reality that lay behind them has changed.'

More positively, Kinnock said that Labour had to come to terms with rising affluence. At one point he attempted to mimic Ron Todd's accent, to the irritation of the transport workers' leader. Two days later Todd retaliated by lampooning Kinnock's own Welsh voice. Todd rounded off a speech on employment law by saying: 'I want to end by quoting from Neil Kinnock, who put it quite clearly when he said: "Look you, Dai. It's about common sense as well as justice, principle as well as pragmatism, Boyo." '

PK

THIS CONFERENCE is dominated by the fact that we meet in the shadow of defeat. Indeed it is that fact which, to all intents and purposes, dominates our agenda, sets our agenda. For we know that out of that defeat we must build victory. We do not therefore go into a period of mourning, for that would be sheer self-indulgence. Instead, we use defeat for its only useful purpose: instruction. We learn from our defeat, and we learn hard enough and deep enough to ensure that it is the last defeat that will be inflicted upon our movement.

That need for learning, that need for instruction, is well understood by this party, as you demonstrated in those overwhelming votes on the review yesterday. There are many lessons to learn and we shall learn them. And as we set about the task I think it is helpful in preparing ourselves for that task of review, of assessment, of analysis, of learning, to remind ourselves without any complacency that there were features of that election which we lost that provide us with foundations of confidence. I say again, without complacency, there were features of that election which meant that, yes, we were defeated, but we certainly were not beaten – certainly not like so many of the commentators and anticipators and watchers of the runes and readers of the tea leaves would have had us believe just weeks before that election started.

Amongst those foundations of confidence is the fact, first, that we significantly increased the number of women Labour MPs – not enough, but a firm step in the right direction. Second, our party achieved the election of four black Members of Parliament, and by that means saw to it that we began to have a multi-racial parliament to reflect our multi-racial society. Third, among these foundations of confidence is the fact that we made very substantial gains in Scotland, Wales and the North of England, and the people who supported us

125

there and everywhere else deserve our thanks and have our thanks. And they have this tribute too: all over this country, all over England, Wales and Scotland, we shall not be taking their support for granted. We regard their support as a spur to greater and more successful efforts, not as any excuse for relaxation.

Fourth, in the foundations of confidence, it is also the case that we did have a very good campaign – not just at the levels that received the most attention and publicity, but, in many ways even more importantly, right through the whole of this party. I want to use this conference to thank people throughout the movement for the unprecedented efforts made everywhere – politically and organisationally – to try to ensure that Labour would win and therefore that Britain would win. That campaign gave people throughout this party energy, pride and confidence. And those feelings stay with us even in defeat. That is important: for it is those qualities of energy, of pride, and of confidence that give this party the courage to be candid, the boldness to be honest, with everyone else and with ourselves.

THE POLICY REVIEW
That is the spirit in which we shall undertake this review; and that was the spirit, I believe, in which the conference took its decision yesterday. That review will be thorough. It will spread across the whole field of policy, leaving nothing out. It will ensure that the programme that we develop in this party is directly related to the conditions that we shall encounter before and during and after the next occasion on which we get the chance to bid for power in a general election. For the task of the review is not to adjust our focus on the past: the task of that review is to give us a clear and accurate perception of the future. The question of whether the policies were right or wrong in June 1987 is of course a matter of some interest – indeed, it is a starting point. But the question of whether the policies will be right or wrong for 1991 must be the matter of the most profound and supreme importance. That is the dominant consideration of that review. That is the frame of mind in which we proceed.

It appears, however, that there are still some who are timid about the idea of 'review'. They seem to have 'do not disturb' notices hung on their minds. The very activity of examination is described by some as a 'betrayal of fundamental principles'. I must say I have a very different opinion of 'review'. I believe that after losing three general election any serious political party that did not undertake the assessment, the review, the examination – and do it honestly – that party would be betraying its principles and its policies and its people.

Indeed I have to say that it is from those people who want us to win that the demand for such a review comes. It has not been dreamt up by Tom Sawyer or by Walworth Road or by the party leadership. Everywhere I have been in the last four months in England, Scotland and Wales I have talked to our party members, talked to the trade unionists, talked to supporters. And anyone who has done the same in our movement will know that it is they who are asking for the review. That demand does not come from people who are defeatist, panic stricken or suffering a political identity crisis. On the contrary, the demand for the review comes from people who are very sure of their political identity, of their ideals, of their principles. So sure, indeed, that they do not think that their convictions will expire like some fragile plant if they are exposed to the light of reality.

These are people who are not afraid to examine, not afraid to think, not afraid to test their beliefs against the realities: because those beliefs were occasioned in the first instance, were rooted, in the realities that they encountered. Indeed, that is the elementary appeal of socialism, that it is related to the realities in which people live their lives. Those people are not the kind of people who would accept, let alone suggest, the discarding of democratic socialist values. And they are not the kind of people who will accept the advice (widely tendered: some of it malicious, some of it merely hysterical) that we should jettison everything we stood for on 11 June, 1987. Nothing would more deserve the charge of cynicism and nothing would more surely sabotage our credibility than to try to make a bonfire of everything that we asked people to vote for in June of this year. So we won't be doing that.

There are two other things that we will not be doing either: we won't be pursuing the pipe dreams of electoral pacts; and we won't be chasing the non-existent pots of political gold at the end of rainbow coalitions. We stand for ourselves, with ourselves and our ideals.

What we will be doing in that process of review, and the activities related to that and many other campaigns, is to develop the means to further the ends of democratic socialism. We shall further the commitments to community, democracy and justice. And to real individual liberty that does not depend for its exercise on the ability of the individual to pay. We shall further the commitments to individual security and freedom from fear, and the commitment to the spread of opportunity to ensure that all people can achieve whatever ability and effort makes possible for them. They are all living purposes. So, too, is the commitment to the civil liberties of every citizen: every man, woman and child, regardless of sex or colour or race or creed. For ours is a socialism that does not just recoil from the ugliness of racism or the insult of sexism; it actively engages itself in combating both on all possible occasions. It is a socialism that knows that the natural environment of this world is fragile; that it is perishable; and that it must be safeguarded against the exploitation and carelessness that constantly menaces the very existence of a habitable environment.

Ours is a socialism, too, that knows that whilst the market is an adequate system for deciding the price and availability of many goods and services, the market has not been, is not, and will never be an adequate mechanism for deciding upon the supply or the quality of health care and education and so much else that is fundamental to a decent life. The market alone will never be adequate for determining the quantity and quality of investment in science or in the arts. And the market alone will never ensure that flow of investment in machines, people, skills and ideas which is necessary to gain and to sustain long-term economic strength and the employment that comes with it. Ours is the kind of socialism which believes that the future will not take care of itself . . . the socialism that holds that preparation for the future cannot be left to the crude short-term calculation of profit and loss, any more than the opportunities and life chances of people can be left just to luck.

They are the values basic to our socialism, basic to the nature of our party. They are the purposes that we want to put into practice. Because there are not declarations, icons or holy relics, these values: they are there as living proposals for the elevation of human kind, the advancement of our whole society. They are there to be put into practice, not into storage. They are the purposes that brought us into this movement and the purposes best able to take us forward in this movement. And we know that, if we are to get the chance to do that (to go forward, to put the purposes into practice), those purposes will have to be matched to the realities that exist and will exist in the coming years. That is common sense. Anyone that does not think it is should heed the advice of Aneurin Bevan who warned that the socialist must be:

On guard against the old words, for the words persist when the reality that lay behind them has changed. It is inherent in our intellectual activity, that we seek to imprison reality in our description of it. Soon, long before we are aware of it, it is we who become the prisoners of the description. From that point on, our ideas degenerate into a kind of folklore which we pass around to each other, fondly thinking we are still talking of the reality around us. We become symbol worshippers. The categories which we once evoked and which once were the tools which we used in our intercourse with reality become hopelessly blunted. In those circumstances the social and political realities we are supposed to be grappling with change and reshape themselves independently of the collective impact of our ideas. We become the creature and no longer the partner of social realities.

That is why I recommend the common sense of realising that we direct and we relate our values, principles and purposes to the realities of our condition, and not to where we would like to be – or to some imagined environment that has yet to be created, indeed yet to be perceptible in the longest possible term. We, in our time, face the challenge of the social realities spoken of by Bevan. We are not daunted by them – such a mood would ill befit any socialist.

SOCIALISM AND AFFLUENCE

The social realities that we face are the realities of increasing home ownership: the realities, too, of less housebuilding and of growing homelessness. We face the fortunate reality of earlier retirement and of longer life for an even larger proportion of the population; and we also face the grim reality of poverty and isolation that so frequently still accompany old age. We face the reality of many more people owning a few shares; and the reality alongside it of increasing poverty, of low pay and growing inequality and division. We face the reality of the change in the pattern of work from mass production manufacturing to high-tech custom production; and, alongside that, too, the reality of under-investment in science and in skills. They are just some of the mixed realities already here or in very firm prospect for the early 1990s – a time in which our economy can no longer rely on the bounty of oil, and there is nothing else left to privatise.

These are just some of the realities we face. They are the realities of a changing economy, a changing society, and they are the realities of a changing electorate too. They present their own fresh challenges, they make their own demands on our candour. If this movement pretends, for instance, that a few million more people owning a few shares each will not make any difference to their perception of their economic welfare then this movement will be fooling itself. Of course, we know that those scattered shares do not make any real difference at all to the structure of economic ownership in our country. They do not make any difference at all to the structure of economic power in our country. But, equally, we know that they do make a difference to their owners' personal economic perceptions. This is a matter of fact. And the result of it is that our policies are going to have to take account of that reality, and of a number of others.

Of course, again, not everyone appears to be willing to listen to that, to understand that. In the past few days I have heard such a recognition of the changing realities described as 'retreat', 'defeatism', 'pandering to yuppies'. It is not a retreat from anything, and it is not pandering to anybody. It is simply understanding the hopes and the doubts, expectations and reservations of people who are not necessarily young, not particularly mobile and who, in any event, did not vote Labour. They are frequently people – not yuppies – who live in the kind of places and work in the kind of jobs that would qualify them for any certificate of working class authenticity that any comrade wanted to award. And they did not vote Labour last time or the time before. Many throughout this movement know them. They know them from their own work, their own families, their own neighbourhood, their canvassing and their campaigning. And those people pose direct questions to us as a socialist movement: they pose questions to us a socialist movement with its direct relationships with trade unions, as a socialist movement that made its appeal across the broad spread of society, that never had any inclination to try and pick and choose who it would like to vote for it. Those people face us with challenges; and we have to recognise those challenges.

Ron Todd made the point with deadly accuracy just a couple of months ago when he asked: 'What do you say to a docker who earns £400 a week, owns his house, a new car, a microwave and a video, as well as a small place near Marbella? You do not say,' said Ron, 'let me take you out of your misery, brother.' When he asked that question, Ron Todd was not suggesting that we trail along in the wake of something called popular capitalism – he was facing a fundamental question for our party with admirable candour that I would recommend universally. It is a question which we must all face if we are going to have an effective response to the changes taking place in our society.

Of course, it is not really a very new question. I remember when I first faced it. It was not last June. It was not in 1983. It was after the 1959 election. I was seventeen and had worked very hard during that election down in the Monmouth constituency. I was devastated, as was the whole movement, not just by defeat but by the scale of our defeat. And I, like just about everyone else in the movement, was asking for explanations of the defeat because it had not felt as though it was going to happen. Amongst the most prominent of those explanations, both in the movement generally and indeed in the annual conference that reviewed the election in that year of 1959, was the assertion that a major reason for our failure in that year, the failure against Macmillan, was something called the Affluent Society. You could hear that everywhere. It was made to sound like a curse. Part of me actually wanted to believe that explanation – it was an easy explanation that had a certain appeal to someone who was convinced that socialism was fundamentally, primarily, a cause that existed to help the underdogs, the downtrodden.

But the other part of me could not really believe that as an explanation. The idea that the Affluent Society, or at least that part of it which I knew, was a bad thing, was contradicted by the evidence of my own eyes – indeed all the experiences of my own living. I could not see for the life of me how it could be that the neighbours' cars that were starting to appear in the street, the wall-to-wall carpeting, the washing machines, the televisions and the first foreign holidays to which the working class were getting access, could somehow be a disadvantage – how could it be anything but a very good thing for the people like my family who had never known anything like that before? And so I could not bring myself to believe that this Affluent Society had thrown such a shadow as to obscure socialism.

I knew that that improvement did not have much to do with Harold Macmillan. I knew where it had come from: people doing lots of very hard work, working overtime, so that they were able to get these things. I could not see either, how those advances were contradictory to the socialism which I believed, and still believe, is about ordinary people getting on: ordinary people having a better life, ordinary people being able to consume more and choose more, and gain greater comfort and opportunity and security. I could not see how socialism was in collision with that. But I was perplexed.

I did what I always did on such occasions when I had these fundamental questions (and you are entitled to do it at any age, but most particularly at that age), I went to see an old socialist in Tredegar, Oliver Jones, and asked him whether there was a collision between affluence and socialism. He told me: 'There is no collision between affluence and socialism – I have been striving for both all my life.' And then he went on to say in words that were unforgettable: 'The point is, you see, that if socialism has got to wait for want, then socialism will wait for a very long time. And it will be right for socialism to wait for a very long time: because if it needs misery to give it majority, God forbid we have the misery.'

He was absolutely right, wasn't he? And it meant then and it means now that democratic socialism has to be as attractive, as beckoning and as useful to the relatively affluent and the relatively secure as it is to the less fortunate in our society who are frequently referred to (in a phrase which I have always thought of as patronising and complacent) as our 'natural vote'. I do not know what that is – I have never known what that is. Any citizen in this democracy who has the right to exercise the franchise is a citizen to whom we should and could be able to make an appeal. That attractiveness and usefulness of democratic socialism should not be difficult for anyone confident about their socialism to be able to demonstrate. It is not a great challenge.

Take the docker of whom Ron spoke, or many others like him earning a little more or a little less. Those kind of people are comfortable, secure, satisfied with decent conditions, and the best of British luck to them. But even with those wages, even with that security, even with that comfort, he is still not able to give the comprehensive care, the special housing, the sheltered accommodation, the support with transport, that his ageing mother and father might need. Even with those wages he is still not getting enough to enable him to meet the price of the schooling for his children, even more so if they wanted to continue into further education or go on to university. And still with those wages, he is not able to ensure that he and his family could meet their full medical needs without worry, especially if there happens to be in that family (as so frequently and tragically is the case) someone with a chronic or crippling illness or disease.

Those are the factors. The way in which the old and the sick are looked after; the kind of serenity people have when they are absolutely sure that they have access to high-quality medical facilities; the unbounded opportunity that we want for our children to ensure that their education should not be cramped by having a price tag attached to it. They are the real assets, and they are the things which condition the quality of life throughout the whole of society. They are the factors which determine the full abundance of life and the real extent of security. And they have something else in common. They are all assets which must be collectively supplied if they are to be there without fail, regardless of the changes of economic fortunes of an individual or the ability to pay.

That commitment, systematic and ready to make that collective provision, cannot come from the current government – or anyone like it – that is guided by hostility to that collective provision. As a matter of doctrine, as a matter of dogma, in the place of that collective provision they want to install a system that makes access to all those assets of care and opportunity increasingly dependent upon the ability to pay. It is a very cheap and a very nasty view, with very expensive and very nasty results. And yet it is presented as an ideological new broom, a compelling doctrine, a grand and radical scheme. A Big Idea taking its place alongside all the great political philosophies. It is called Thatcherism, the Big Idea.

THATCHERISM'S FAILURES

What is this Big Idea? How is it attuned to the realities, how does it stand up to the examination of real circumstances? How, for instance, does the Big Idea address the real problems of a generation of children who will meet greater challenges in their future as citizens and workers than any generation has ever known before? Well, the Big Idea responds to that reality and the responsibilities for that generation by making such cuts in education investment as to put education spending as a proportion of our GNP lower than that of any comparable economy.

What has the Big Idea got for the inner cities? It has a galaxy of initiatives, programmes, task forces and schemes – in fact it has everything except money. The Big Idea, applied to the inner city, is that you put one pound of programme money in for every nine pounds that you take out in rate support grant from the inner cities. That is the Big Idea. The Big Idea cuts investment in house building by three quarters in eight years. And the Big Idea now requires the imposition of a poll tax – a tax which has no connection with ability to pay, which punishes families which have dependent sick or aged relatives or dependent grown up children at home, which costs a fortune to administer and which tears up the roots of local democracy. That is the Big Idea.

Then there is the jewel in the crown of this great new intellectual and ideological force. The jewel in the crown of the Big Idea: privatisation. The sell-off system which is supposed to be the engine of popular capitalism, but which turns out to be a scheme for changing great public monopolies into great private monopolies by means which ensure that some small investors get a little slice of gain and a few very big investors get great slabs of additional wealth and the power that goes with it. Private monopolies cannot deliver an efficient telephone system, but are excellent, brilliant, magnificent as a means of handing over major British assets to foreign asset holders. A scheme of privatisation which turned Jaguar Cars into an American-owned company, a scheme of privatisation which is turning Rolls Royce into a Japanese concern, a scheme of privatisation which is just about to turn British Petroleum into anything but British.

Now of course we have another of the ideologues, John Moore. He has the Big Idea: 'To move people away from dependency,' as he put it, 'and towards opportunity'. It sounds very attractive, does it not, opportunity? My father used to say that he was brought up in an opportunity society – boundless opportunities, opportunities everywhere you looked. And he said that the only thing that made him as one of seven children go down the pit at fourteen was sheer bloody-mindedness! Move away from dependency towards opportunity – it does sound like a good idea. Nobody likes the status of dependence. The human taste is always for self reliance: indeed, that is a major, basic reason for our advocacy of socialism, to be able to extend that self reliance so that people do not have to be dependent.

Our way of doing it, of course, is to end dependence by trying to end need. Mr Moore works from the other direction. He intends to end dependence by ending provision: teaching people to fly by pushing them off the roof – that is how he wants to end dependence! And that is his Big Idea: you are on your own. What a brilliant new idea! What a forceful and compelling way to have our society ruled.

Can the Big Idea attend to the real basics? That should be very easy for such a great scheme. Can it, for instance, attend to the very rudimentary requirements of old and poor people to keep warm in the winter? No, it can't. Not because of any malevolence or meanness, you understand, but because these saintly enemies of dependence would simply not want to demean frightened and freezing old people with the status of being 'dependants'. They are kindness themselves, you know, these ideologues of the Big Idea.

The Big Idea is not just applied at home. The same small mindedness applied abroad too. For when asked to tackle any of the great issues of menace to the environment, of racial oppression, of want in the world – that Big Idea turns in upon itself and shrinks into selfishness. It is a Big Idea that will not join in any of the international initiatives to combat the poisoning of the land, the sea or the air. It is a Big Idea that will accommodate and appease apartheid and refuse to tighten sanctions to squeeze down on that regime on the grounds, as the prime minister puts it, of morality. Morality, when the object of those sanctions should be a government of apartheid that is allowing the imprisonment, torture, beating and killing of children who are said to threaten their apartheid state in their protests against it. It is a Big Idea that cuts the aid budget in half and turns its back on the people of the world who need some extra help to enable them to make their way out of the misery of poverty, insecurity and starvation. How can anything so empty of responsibility, so empty of generosity, of decency, be thought to be a Big Idea?

DISARMAMENT

There are Big Ideas around. I'll tell you who has got a really Big Idea. Gorbachev and Reagan, Shevardnadze and Shultz, they have a Big Idea. They have a really Big Idea. Their Big Idea is to secure the withdrawal of intermediate nuclear forces and then to embark upon significant reduction in strategic nuclear weapons. Now that is what I call a really Big Idea.

That is a major purpose: but too major, it would appear, for this government in Britain; and that is why they have tried to block every stride in all the progress made since Reykjavik, laying across the path of progress all the time. Friendly visits to Washington, little nips into Europe, speeches from the Berlin wall, speeches that collide with those who have the Big Idea. George Shultz, the American Secretary of State, when challenged that the removal of intermediate weapons would not bring about a vast reduction in the nuclear stockpiles on each side, said that that was true. But, he said: 'We have to start somewhere'. Within days, the response of the mistress of the Big Idea is not to say: 'Yes, let us make a start, let us see what we can get and how far we can mutually go.' It is to say, in her words: 'It has gone far enough.' What a Big Idea.

But of course she is wrong. Because the patent fact about the attitude of the superpowers is that they consider that the progress has not gone far enough. And we, like the huge majority of humanity, agree with them entirely in that view, that the progress has not gone far enough. There is a long course yet to run. We welcome the fact that the process will continue, and, as it continues, will change and improve the condition of common security in this world. Not only in the nuclear sphere, but in securing the ending of chemical weapons and the reduction and balance of non-nuclear conventional forces. We welcome that process. And because of the continued assertions on both sides of a real will to proceed, we can look forward to that improvement in common security. That is why we will work to ensure that we have policies that are capable of dealing with the changed conditions of the 1990s in a way that will enhance the prospect of removing reliance on nuclear weapons of any description.

'YEARS, NOT WEEKS'

In that, and in many other ways, we shall review our policies. Those reviews will take their direction and their inspiration from the values of compassion and concern. They will show our commitment to Britain and the British people. They will be sharpened on the realities: including the salient fact of life that – if we are to achieve our ambitions of proper care, of full opportunity, of defeating poverty and disadvantage – we must implement policies to make our economy more competitive, more efficient, more productive. That is essential, for without it we could not fulfil our contract to generate jobs, or to meet social needs, or to modernise and multiply the essential services of health and education.

Of course, all our enemies and, yes, some of our friends give the impression that we are hostile to those ideas of efficiency and competitiveness – just as we are said to be antagonistic to personal good fortune, to private industry and to a lot of other things. But if any of that were the case, why is it that so many of our members and supporters are buying their houses, so many of our members and supporters are making personal pension arrangements, and undertaking many other activities to secure proper protection for themselves and their families? If we really had those hostilities, why would so many Labour councils (to their eternal credit) show such initiative and expend such energy on attracting and retaining and working in partnership with so much private industry? If we really had that opposition to efficiency and competition, why would so many of our trade union colleagues scourge management for under-investment, for inadequate provision for training, for poor sales promotion and marketing activities?

The truth is, is it not, that so frequently and so rightly, when we get the chance to improve the material well-being of our families, our communities, our colleagues in this movement, we take that chance. And we are right to do so. When local councillors of this party can win industrial development for their areas, they do it. When trade unionists can secure the advantage of the members of their union by more efficient performance, they do it. There is no concession of ideals in that. Certainly there is no corruption of the values of socialism or its purposes. There is nothing to apologise for: indeed, they are personal and collective achievements, by socialists, for socialist purposes. So – instead of tolerating the insults of our enemies, or accommodating the indulgence of a few of our friends, that we are, or somehow should be, antagonistic to material advance – we would really be better employed telling the truth about ourselves, employed best of all in ensuring that we preach what, in reality, we are practising. And then perhaps we would get some credit for it where credit is due.

That is the spirit in which we will review and renew our economic policies to ensure that we develop the strategy necessary to meet our economic and social goals. That is our purpose; and we shall accomplish it. And then we shall promote it. And we shall promote it in 'years not weeks'. That, of course, must be our well-developed habit in every area. In the last few months I have heard the phrase 'years not weeks' very frequently. I needed no persuasion. For, as it happens, I had the chance – indeed the duty – to say it first: elections are won in years, not weeks. I did not just have the chance and the duty to say it on the night of our election defeat in June of this year, but I actually said it in the plainest possible terms, as some of you may recall, from this very platform when you elected me leader four years ago: 'Elections are won in years, not weeks.' Many listened, many understood, many applied it; and they have worked to win for 'years, not weeks' right throughout this movement. That is why, in the last four years, we have been engaged in continual campaigning: the NHS campaign; the *Freedom and Fairness* campaign; the *Investing in People* campaign; the *Jobs and Industry* campaign; the *Modern Britain in a Modern World* campaign; and a host of other campaigns at national and local level. All for the purpose of trying to secure an advance in years and not in weeks.

There were many who understood that the need to work 'for years not weeks' applied not only to the obligation of campaigning in this party, but to conduct in this party as well. They understood that we would be judged not only by the substance of policies or the quality of campaigns, but also by the way in which we acted as people and as a party. Now, in the wake of our third election defeat, there can be very few, if there be any at all, who do not comprehend the need to be convincing in all three of those areas: policy, campaigning and conduct. All three, and we forget them at our peril.

To maintain all three will require self-discipline. The self-discipline of not promising so much that the promise is destroyed by incredibility. The self-discipline of understanding the implications of action. Not just for the short term, not just in the immediate situation but for the standing of the whole movement, wherever that action is taken. The self-discipline of ensuring that every word, every deed, every statement, every action, is related completely to the task of achieving victory. The self-discipline of accepting that in everything that each of us, individually and collectively, says and does, we work in the clear and certain knowledge that we address many people who still need to be convinced if they are to make the shift to supporting us – people who need to be certain that their trust in our common purpose and in our common sense is fully justified.

None of that means speaking of our socialism behind cupped hands. None of that self-discipline and sacrifice means bowing down to prejudice or injustice. It does not mean putting away our initiatives and it does not mean forgetting our inspirations. Recognising those requirements of a serious, sensible, socialist movement is not defeatism, nor is it a retreat from convictions. On the contrary, recognising it and applying it is the precondition of the victory which we need to get the power to put those convictions into effect.

That is not a plea for self-discipline. I am not pleading at all. Because the people who need us are not pleading. The people who need us are demanding – demanding that we conduct our affairs, run our movement, meet our responsibilities to each other and to the community. And meet those responsibilities in such a way as to continually demonstrate those qualities of vitality, purpose and unity which brought us such credit during the election campaign.

When that demand for unity is made, I anticipate the question: 'unity on whose terms?' And the answer is, on the terms of the people who support us and would like to support us. For serious socialists, for serious democrats, that is not much to ask. And if anyone doubts the need for that self-discipline, for that unity, then they had better just remind themselves of the price that is paid for indiscipline and disunity. It is not paid by those who are locked in combat, it is not paid by those who have an interesting exchange, it is not paid by those who thrive on division. The price is paid by the people of Britain. And it is paid most by those who need most: those who need the schools and the homes, those who need the hospitals, those who need chances for themselves that can only be built on the foundations of a just society and a strong economy. The price for division and disunity is paid most of all by those who attract our greatest concern, those who most need our help, those who most depend upon our success. We cannot let them down, we must not let them pay that price again.

That is why we review. That is why we reassess. That is why we regroup. They are acts of rededication to our principles and our purposes, and to policies that are attuned to the realities in which people live. They are the acts of a party that is not satisfied with the luxury of opposition or attracted by the purity of powerlessness. They are the acts of a party that cannot live on constant diets of resolutions condemning and motions deploring and statements opposing, when it wants the power to do things. It is the act of rededication, the act of a party that knows that it will offer nothing to the British people if it contents itself with gestures that will be ignored, bluffs that will be called and illegality that will be ruthlessly punished.

Review, reassessment, regrouping are the acts of a party that wants power to decide, power to influence, power to govern in a way that can advance the condition of our fellow human beings. We seek the opportunities of that power and accept the obligations of that power. Of course they will impose pressures and impose burdens. But ask anyone in this movement: who is not prepared to accept such responsibilities? Whether they want this party to achieve victory, or whether they will settle for being members of a party that can offer the British people nothing but sympathy? A party that will do little more than attend the funerals of hopes and of communities and of industries, a party of permanent condolence senders. I do not think that that is what this party and its members want for themselves or accept for themselves.

Comrades, four years ago when you elected me leader I told you that there must be no activity in this Labour movement superior to that of defeating Toryism. I meant every word. I meant no activity superior to that task of defeating Toryism. I say it again. I know that there are now many more people in this movement who not only understand that to be desirable but regard it as essential and act upon it all the time. That is now the spirit in the Labour movement in its overwhelming majority. And because that is the spirit, it makes us fit to fight. It makes us fit to win. And it will make us fit to govern.

1988
BLACKPOOL

'No such thing as society?'

In March 1988 Tony Benn announced his decision to challenge Neil Kinnock for the party leadership; Eric Heffer mounted a parallel challenge to Roy Hattersley for the deputy leadership. This move was designed to rally the Left against any dilution of Labour's policies. Although nobody expected Benn or Heffer to win, a large vote might frighten the leadership enough to curb its more revisionist ambitions.

In the event, the Benn/Heffer challenge marginalised the Left still further, and enhanced Kinnock's authority. Four MPs resigned from the Campaign Group in protest at the challenge: Margaret Beckett, Jo Richardson, Joan Ruddock and Clare Short. Benn succeeded in opening up debate among local activists about Labour's overall direction; but the result of that debate was the opposite of what he had intended. Party members inspected the rival prospectuses and overwhelmingly chose Kinnock's. When the results of the leadership election were announced on 2 October, the first evening of the party conference, Kinnock had won 88.6 per cent support, and Benn only 11.4 per cent. Among constituency parties – where Benn had hoped to win significant support – Kinnock's margin of victory was more than four-to-one.

The deputy leadership contest was complicated by the presence of a third candidate, John Prescott. His opposition to Hattersley had more to do with style than politics: He thought the deputy leader should be more active within the party, building up its membership and reviving its organisation. Prescott insisted that his campaign should not be regarded as hostile to Kinnock; however it was widely seen in precisely that light. When the votes were counted, Hattersley had 66.8 per cent support, Prescott 23.7 and Heffer 9.5.

The leadership contest helped Kinnock; but the progress of Labour's internal debate on defence policy was less happy. On 5 June

Kinnock was interviewed on BBC1's Sunday lunchtime politics programme, 'This Week, Next Week'. He appeared to edge away from his previous non-nuclear stance: 'There is no need now for a something-for-nothing unilateralism. The idea that there is a something-for-nothing thrust that can be made is redundant.' With encouragement from Kinnock's office, the media interpreted this as the first public sign that Labour's defence policy was likely to change.

The interview provoked a furious, if predictable, row. What was less predictable – and more worrying for Kinnock – was the way that row threatened to heal the fracture that Kinnock had nurtured so carefully within the Left. Robin Cook and David Blunkett were two of the MPs who had done most to line up most of the Left behind Kinnock and so isolate the Campaign Group. But both men were angered by Kinnock's words and sought a retraction. Among other things, they feared that Benn's leadership campaign might gather momentum. Kinnock's problems were compounded by Denzil Davies's decision a week later to resign as shadow defence secretary. Davies did not object to a change of policy as such; he complained, rather, that Kinnock never consulted him.

On 20 June, Kinnock went to lunch at the *Independent*. Normally such occasions are off-the-record, but at Kinnock's insistence this discussion was on-the-record, and tape recorded. Pressed to clarify his defence policy, he reverted to the formula he had used in the 1987 general election campaign: he remained a unilateralist, and if Labour won the next election he would immediately decommission Britain's nuclear weapons. The next morning's *Independent* published Kinnock's responses verbatim. His reverse somersault dismayed the party's multilateralists and provoked mockery in the media; but in the short term it did at least prevent Benn and Heffer from adding to their support on the Left.

By the time Kinnock came to deliver his conference speech, he had won the leadership election conclusively. The process of edging Labour away from unilateralism could continue. It was, however, clear that the change would have to be handled more deftly than the summer's television interview and newspaper lunch. Careful reading of Kinnock's speech showed that he reopened the door to change, but in a way that did not frighten the pro-Kinnock, anti-Benn sections of Labour's left wing.

Kinnock's 1988 speech signalled change in another part of Labour's international policy. At the 1983 general election, Labour's manifesto had advocated Britain's withdrawal from the European Community. Its 1987 manifesto indicated wary acceptance of EC membership, while continuing to 'reject EC interference with our policy for national recovery and renewal'.

That policy could not easily be reconciled with moves to complete the EC's internal market and the prospects for monetary union. After Labour's defeat, a new policy was inevitable – not least because by the time Labour would next have a chance to form a government, the final arrangements for the single market would largely be settled.

If there was one moment when the dominant attitude of Britain's Labour movement towards Europe switched from caution to enthusiasm, it was when Jacques Delors, the president of the European Commission, addressed the Trades Union Congress in Bournemouth in September 1988. Delors told the TUC that he wanted the EC to develop a 'social dimension', in which workers' rights would be protected throughout the community:

> 1992 is much more than the creation of an internal market abolishing barriers to the free movement of goods, services, and investment. In my opinion social dialogue and collective bargaining are essential pillars of our democratic society.

Delors invited trade unionists to be the 'architects of Europe'. His speech won immediate support from most unions and Labour politicians, not least because it offered a strategy that managed to be both pro-European and anti-Conservative. Kinnock's conference speech four weeks later developed this approach, and marked the beginning of his attempt to portray the Labour leadership as more committed Europeans than the Conservatives.

Europe was not the only issue where Kinnock sought to wrest the initiative from the Conservatives. The week before the 1988 conference, Thatcher had made a widely publicised speech to the Royal Society, where she argued that the greenhouse effect and the threats to the ozone layer had not been fully appreciated. She warned that humankind had 'begun a massive experiment with the system of the planet itself'. New policies, she said, would be needed 'for energy production, for fuel efficiency and for reforestation'. Kinnock's speech in Blackpool was his first opportunity to respond.

PK

145

NOW THAT everyone has had an opportunity to digest the results of Sunday night, I should like to thank you again for your support. You know that my feeling about the leadership election was that it was an unneccesary distraction from our work in the party. But the fact is, asked for or not, elections have results and results give mandates. That mandate was given democratically and it will be used democratically. It will be used very deliberately and very directly for the purpose for which I believe it was given to me by people right across the Labour movement. The purpose of unity. The purpose of change. The purpose of doing everything that can be done to secure victory for this party at the next general election. That is why I was given this mandate. I was given the mandate, too – and this is how I will serve it – in order to pursue the democratic socialist values of this movement and the social and economic vision which arises from those values.

JUSTICE AND EFFICIENCY

We are socialists, we are rationalists. Our vision is insight, not a mirage. We have strong ideals, but our idealism is not naïvety. We do not pretend the world is as it is not. We have a dream, but we are not dreamers. We do not simply desire ends. We understand the necessity of committing means and it is precisely that which produces our commitment to social justice and to economic efficiency.

There are those, of course, like the present government, who consider social justice to be an impediment to economic efficiency. There are some – including, from what they say, some in our movement – who consider economic efficiency to be a threat to social justice. Both are wrong. The simple fact is that sustained social justice depends upon a foundation of economic prosperity and economic

146

success cannot be properly achieved without social justice. Justice and efficiency – the two go together.

Of course, you can get some costs down, you can get some profits up, you can get some form of efficiency by ignoring social justice. You can say that you are slimming down, sharpening up, shaking out, and call it efficiency. But if in the process you shut down 30 per cent of your country's manufacturing capacity, if you refuse to modernise training or invest in science, if you have generated all the costs and losses of mass unemployment, if you have kept your interest rates and your currency at a level which helps importers and harms exporters, then the efficiency you get is going to be limited, fragile and temporary.

Similarly, you can – and should – have greater justice out of better distribution. You can – and should – use what you have got more fairly. You can – and should – take the most from those who are best off and give the most to those who are worst off. All that is essential. But it is not enough by itself. Unless the policies of justice and generosity are built on the foundation of vitality of production, efficiency of production, expansion of production, they will not last very long. Those policies of justice and generosity will die for lack of sustenance, lack of means. Justice and efficiency. They are inter-dependent.

The proof of that abounds. Education and training provide the most obvious examples. That is not recognised in practice by a government whose commitment to training is a fraction of that of our competitors. It is not recognised at all by a government whose education policy is to opt out schools under a cabinet that has altogether opted out of state education. They refuse to recognise that you cannot have an efficient economy if you waste the potential of the people. And you cannot have a fair society either. If we want fairness and efficiency, we shall, for instance, have to break the historic habit of regarding girls and women as second class citizens in so many spheres of education, training and employment. We shall have to stop treating child-bearing and child-rearing as a disqualification from opportunities. We shall have to stop treating the provision of childcare as a privilege and a luxury and start to treat it as a right and a necessity. And if, in this modern economy with the changing shape of its workforce and the changing conditions, demands and realities of work, we are to ensure that women have the opportunity to reach their full potential, part-time workers must have full-time rights when it comes to training, social security support and health and safety at work.

Justice argues for that. So does efficiency. For there is no stimulus to advance in poverty wages, low skills, bad conditions, exploitation, insecurity. All of those are an inducement to employers not to make the commitment to investment, modernisation and development. It is folly for anybody to assume that you can secure economic success in a low-tech, no tech, low-wage economy. That is the opposite of justice and the opposite of efficiency for both sexes. And it doesn't work. That is the test that we apply. Not just in our criticism and condemnation of the sweatshop, but in our judgment in the whole shape of the economy.

For some people, judgment of the shape of the economy is very easy. There are those, like the government, who simply say 'private good, public bad'. There are those who say, in a mirror image, 'public good, private bad'. Neither of them are dealing with the realities. Neither of them are applying the real test, the real judgment of the shape and performance of industry. Neither are asking the real question 'does it work?'. But that test *is* applied elsewhere. It is applied in Germany, in Japan, in Sweden, in France. In all of those countries they appreciated long ago that public and private sectors, government and market, had to work *in combination* if the strength of the economy was to be developed and the potential of the economy to be maximised. It is that combination that works.

We have to make it work for us in Britain through all the instruments available. Through social ownership in all its forces, great and small. Through regulation to protect consumers, the environment, health and safety conditions both of workers and – we remind ourselves in this year of the King's Cross disaster – of the public as well. We must use the instruments of strategic investment in training, in science, in research and development. All of that is essential to strengthening a British economy that is underinvested, underperforming and carrying a huge trade deficit. Some of those weaknesses are chronic. Some are acute and recent. They've come about despite the enormous oil bonus. The weaknesses would be serious in any circumstances. They would present great challenges at any time. But now we are facing the extra pressure and contests that arise from the completion of the European Community single market.

The Tories' preparation for that huge change has been pathetically inadequate. It has consisted of a £9 million advertising campaign and a few business breakfasts. For the Tories the single market is nothing more than a free capital market. They ignore industry's needs – whether those needs are for modern training support, for science funding or for a competitive pound to give our exporters a fighting chance in the rest of the European Community. Patently, our producers have not had that chance. When Margaret Thatcher became Prime Minister in 1979 we had a balance of payments surplus with the remainder of the European Community of nearly £1 billion. But what is not advertised as we approach that single market is that we now have a deficit with the other countries of the European Community of £14 billion. In those circumstances, we patently have not been prepared, we are patently at a disadvantage, made all the greater by the fact that our major competitors in the Community market have been making strategic preparation, sector by sector preparation, industry by industry preparation, to see what advantage they can secure.

Apart from the absence of preparation, the government resent and resist the *social* obligations arising from the creation of the single market. It is the hostility to that social dimension which has produced the Prime Minister's play acting in recent weeks. This is the Prime Minister who whipped and guillotined the Single European Act through the House of Commons in 1985 specifically to spur the move to the single market. So it is no good her playing Boadicea now when she sold the pass three years ago. The intensity of Margaret Thatcher's hostility to the very concept of the social dimension disgusts even Conservatives in Europe. They should understand that the very idea of 'community' makes Margaret Thatcher recoil.

Our attitude is very different. We want Europe to be a community as well as a market. We want that market to work for people, not the other way round. We want continuing common strategies for expansion across the Community in place of the Eurosclerosis that leaves eighteen million workers in that single market unemployed. And we want all that because we insist on social justice as well as economic efficiency. That insistence is put by democratic socialists right across the continent. In the TUC last month, Jacques Delors said: 'The European Community will be characterised by co-operation as well as competition. It will encourage individual initiative as well as

149

solidarity. It would be unacceptable for Europe to become a source of social regression, while we are trying to rediscover together the road to prosperity and employment.' Of course, Delors was right.

If a single market is created that extends across half the continent of Europe and the requirements of social justice are not installed as a central component in that venture, then the fruits of economic efficiency will be scooped up by a few countries – indeed, a few regions in a few countries. We will then be left with two Europes: rich and poor, congested and neglected, over-developed and under-developed – and I mean under-developed in the most literal sense. None of that would be just. Certainly, none of it would be efficient. It would be expensive, ugly, a constant cause of waste, a constant source of tensions between peoples. That is why we say that the social dimension of the single market must be central to the prospectus and to the practice of the European Community.

Social Europe must mean getting the highest standards of working conditions and workers' rights right across that single market. It must mean raising pensions and benefits to European standards. British pensioners will know how far they lag behind their contemporaries in the rest of the European Community. It is a source of shame. It must mean, in this multinational market, tough anti-trust laws firmly enforced by domestic governments and by the Community itself in order to protect the consumer against monopoly and monopoly practices. It must mean substantial social and regional funds to counteract the market's inevitable pull of wealth, production and jobs towards the centre. And social Europe must mean the root and branch reform of the Common Agricultural Policy which is unsustainable in terms of justice and efficiency.

PROTECTING THE ENVIRONMENT

It is clear, too, in this neighbourhood of Europe, where distances get smaller and contact gets greater, where the idea of community with diversity gets clearer, that we live cheek by jowl and social Europe must mean community action to safeguard, to protect and conserve the environment: land, sea and air. In the name of social justice and economic efficiency we insist upon all of that. Nowhere is that insistence stronger than in policy on the environment. Perhaps, here at least is some conjunction with the Prime Minister after her speech last week. She is aroused to the environment. It took many people so much by surprise that there was talk of administering a drug test!

The arousal has been a long time coming. She has had nine years of power. Nine years in which the hazardous waste imported into this country has increased tenfold because the British government of Margaret Thatcher has kept standards of monitoring, checking and storage so low that firms in Britain can actually undercut firms in the remainder of the European Community. In her nine years of power the government has consistently weakened and blocked European moves to control industrial emissions and to improve the quality of water in the reservoirs, rivers and in the sea around our coasts. In her nine years of power, the National Environmental Research Council has had its grant cut. So much so that a scientist, commenting last week on Mrs Thatcher's remarks said: 'To be a scientist in Britain now is to know what it felt like to be a Christian in ancient Rome.'

Perhaps after the speech to the Royal Society last week the sinner repenteth. And we, being generous spirits, will rejoice – not necessarily in heaven but in Blackpool – which is the next best thing, I am told. If the sinner repenteth, if there really is a change, we welcome it. But if there really is a change of heart it produces a basic question that Mrs Thatcher must answer. She must tell us and the country how she thinks it is possible to protect the local, the national, the international environment from the poisoning and pillaging now going on by relying on the mechanisms of the market which she so much admires. How will it be possible for that to be done? If she is going to rely solely or mainly on the willingness of the market to tend to the great strategic issues of cleaning and conserving the environment, then the lady is not serious.

To be serious she will have to respond to the calls that we have made together with Greenpeace, SERA, Friends of the Earth and many other lobbies and bodies anxious to conserve and develop, improve and protect the environment. We have made calls for investment in science, more prosaic calls for the repair of the sewers of Britain, calls for cleaning up the beaches, controlling the industrial filth that is thrown into the sky and into the sea because there is totally inadequate control. If the Prime Minister really is serious about her commitment, she will have to respond to the repeated calls for urgent action and new legislation to control pesticides, to control the import of waste, to control and prevent dumping at sea and to reduce atmospheric pollution. The Prime Minister can soon produce tangible proof of her intent. She can incorporate all of those demands that I listed and a few more in the Queen's Speech next month. She can make the absolute commitment to comprehensive legislation. She can do it very quickly. We would support that legislation gladly. We want it, we have argued for it.

We want some answers to some questions as well: since the Prime Minister claims such zeal for the protection of the environment, is she going to introduce new regulations to stop the development sprawl into the green belt in the south-east and elsewhere in Britain? Is she going to stop Ridley's raiders spraying concrete over this green and pleasant land? For it is a fact that her successive secretaries of state for the environment have softened, dissolved, effectively removed the assortment of circulars and regulations that gave communities the right to protect themselves against speculative development and urban sprawl. They, in the name of the market, have taken that away. If the Prime Minister is serious, for the sake of consistency, she will not just have to restore powers that previously existed, she will have to make them modern and absolute as we would.

The Prime Minister has another question to answer. Is she going to provide local authorities with new resources, extra rate support grant, for urban improvement instead of punishing those local authorities who have tried to do their best to protect, develop and improve their urban environment? You cannot be an environment enthusiast and a ratecapper. Is she going to cancel water privatisation? Surely, anyone so evangelical about the environment as the Prime Minister could not possibly contemplate handing the supply and safety of water to owners who are only going to consider quality *after* they have decided what profit they need to take.

Is the Prime Minister going to cancel electricity privatisation? Surely, anyone with her fervour about the environment could not possibly transfer control over nuclear energy, over the burning of fossil fuels, over the conditions of production and supply and price to owners of the industry who, by definition, will have to put profit first. Surely, no one with her newfound fervour for safeguarding the environment of Britain could contemplate any act of privatisation that would result in the extensive ownership and control of water and electricity – two fundamentals of life – to commercial interests that either do not belong to this country or are not interested in this country or both. How can that kind of control be handed to people who will never have to live with the consequences?

There is, of course, one other great requirement for anyone expressing serious concern about the environment. It is that they do everything possible to ensure that the poor countries of the world – the poor countries whose poverty itself is a major cause of environmental degradation – are helped out of their agony. If Margaret Thatcher is going to do that, the very least she has to do is to double the current level of overseas development aid, for her government, in nine years, have cut it in half.

Mrs Thatcher has been to Africa. Geoffrey Howe has been to the north Kenyan desert. So it is not as if they have not witnessed the consequences of people so poor that they have actually got to kill the earth from which they live, by over-grazing, over-farming, without any adequate support, without adequate investment, without adequate tools, without irrigation. The land is so over-used that they know that in the very act of feeding their families today they are beckoning famine for their families tomorrow. That has not happened because of carelessness. It has not happened because of incompetence. These are some of the most skilled farmers in the world – most of them women, naturally. It has happened because of the intensity of cultivation that they had been forced into because of their poverty. If Margaret Thatcher is serious about the world's environment, as she said, if she thinks that it is 'the great challenge' of the last part of this century and of the next century, she has got to provide money to ensure that people can save their lives and the lives of their families by having the resources to care for the earth that feeds them. If she did that it would be social justice and economic efficiency on a global scale.

THATCHER'S VALUES
We need that in our international relationships just as much as we need it in our national life. For if social justice and economic efficiency are not the ruling values of our society, where does our society go? Many people are asking that. They say: 'What is happening to our country and what is going to happen to our country?' Anne Holmes is here. She was our candidate in Kensington. People who had never voted Labour before voted Labour because they were asking this question as they witnessed the great divide – not the north-south divide, the south-south divide that fractures the south of Britain as Britain is divided north to south. These were prosperous people

concerned about what was happening in their society around them and what is happening to our country.

The answer is that unless we apply the policies of social justice and economic efficiency to create wealth, and unless we apply those policies to use that wealth to create a fairer society in Britain, then Britain inevitably goes further along the path that it is set upon now. It goes further along the path to a split society. It goes further towards a community divided into three unequal parts – a small, opulent superclass at the top; a larger class of people living in a reasonable but sometimes anxious affluence in the middle – especially those at the bottom end of that central class who are subject to the pressures of a credit-driven economy; and at the bottom a third class, an underclass of people living in dire need. I am not describing some distant tomorrow, some awful decade away, I am describing Britain now. In Britain now nearly nine million men, women and children live on supplementary benefit. Another nine million live on low pay. That is one in three of the population, eighteen million people on poverty level whether they earn those desperately low wages or are thrust into poverty because of unemployment, illness or disability and are confined to the dependence on what the government chooses to hand out to them in their social security system.

By 1991, that underclass will be even bigger – twenty-two million men, women and children – and they suffer all of the social and civil disadvantages that go with their low incomes. Our society is disfigured and endangered by such great poverty. To their credit, many who are not poor understand that. They understand, too, that a society with such great and growing differences in personal economic conditions is unlikely to be a society at peace with itself. It is an insecure society. That is what we have now.

The expressions of insecurity take many forms. They include increasing family break-up, increasing neurotic stress and break-down, poverty and homelessness, crimes of sexual abuse and robbery, drug and alcohol abuse, a huge rise in violence for criminal ends and – incredibly and terrifyingly – a spread in violence for entertainment, whether it is in football crowds or in quiet country towns on a Saturday night. Of course, no one could or would blame the government for all that. But it is impossible to accept that there is no connection between the fracturing of our society and the grabbing 'loadsamoney' ethic encouraged by a government that treats care as 'drooling', compassion as 'wet'. A government led by a Prime Minister who says that: 'There is no such thing as society.'

'No such thing as society,' she says.

No obligation to the community.

No sense of solidarity.

No principles of sharing or caring.

'No such thing as society.'

No sisterhood, no brotherhood.

No neighbourhood.

No honouring other people's mothers and fathers.

No succouring other people's little children.

'No such thing as society.'

No number other than one.

No person other than me.

No time other than now.

No such thing as society, just 'me' and 'now'.

That is Margaret Thatcher's society.

I tell you, you cannot run a country on the basis of 'me' and 'now.'

You cannot run domestic policy on that basis, and you certainly cannot run international policy on that basis. Nowhere is that more obvious than in defence policies. Margaret Thatcher tries to operate 'me' and 'now' policies at every level. Thankfully, other leaders do not share her narrowness or her lack of vision.

The relationship between the superpowers has been changing radically since Reykjavik. But it is in the year since we last met at conference that that changed relationship has manifested itself in tangible form, with the treaty to remove intermediate nuclear weapons. That relationship, whatever the outcome of the presidential elections in the United States of America, will be further developed by the reduction in strategic nuclear arms and it will be strengthened by agreements on conventional force reductions.

Those changes have taken place partly because of the fact that Mikhail Gorbachev and – I guess you never thought you would hear it from this platform – Ronald Reagan, too, had the courage and wisdom to take initiatives that grew, according to their own testimony, from the fact that they as individuals and as leaders, they have accepted the moral arguments against nuclear weapons that we, and many like us across the world, have been putting for three decades and more. When Mikhail Gorbachev and Ronald Reagan say that we have

155

'entered the age of nuclear disarmament', then there are opportunities for clearing countries and continents of nuclear weapons that have not existed at any time since NATO and the Warsaw Pact became nuclear powers. That is why we must encourage all new steps, celebrate all new achievements and seek the power to participate in that process to end dependence on nuclear weapons anywhere in the world. That is what we must do.

That power, as is obvious to everyone, can only be attained, only be exercised in government. For everyone here and throughout the Labour movement knows that if we do not get the power of government, the consequence will be that Trident will definitely be completed and deployed, and, in addition, other systems will be multiplied under the guise of 'modernisation'. To win power is to have the means of achieving a non-nuclear defence policy ourselves and securing the reduction in the nuclear weapons systems of others. Not to win power is to make certain the increase of nuclear arms by a Tory government that wants more of such arms and not less. This party, I am certain, wants to be part of the process of nuclear disarmament. Indeed, this party wants to take a leading part in that process of nuclear disarmament. That is only possible in government. It is not possible out of government.

When we conclude our review next year and when we resolve our policy for fighting the next General Election, that policy must be serious about nuclear disarmament, serious about defence. Indeed, so serious about both objectives that we are capable of earning the democratic power to achieve them.

SOCIALISM AND INDIVIDUALISM

The whole policy review process is a challenge that we have given ourselves. Many welcome it and participate in it as a means of refining and refreshing the ways of applying our values in practice. Others are not so bold. They see the emphasis on individualism and on competitiveness and it sends them reaching for their slogans: 'We don't like all that talk about individualism,' they say.

Frankly, I am amazed that any socialist can say that. Because to me there is no test for progress *other* than its impact on the individual. The great inspiration, the great distinction of democratic socialism is that it does not just desire the ends of individual liberty, individual identity, individual choice, it actually commits itself to collectively providing the means for the people to exercise their rights in practice. Let those who say that there is a collision between concern for the individual and commitment to collective provision understand this – that the whole purpose of such collective provision is the service, the safety, the care, the opportunity of the individual. For democratic socialists, collective provision is a means not an end. The moment that the collective becomes an end in itself, a basic value is deserted and socialists deliver themselves into the hands of those who want to defame socialism as a creed of uniformity, of regimentation, of drab levelling down.

We want none of those things. Our belief is in diversity, liberty, real freedom of choice and real freedom of chance, real freedoms that can be exercised because the means exist and are at the disposal of every person for the material and spiritual advance of all people. Be confident in that belief. The collective is the means not the end, and the end is the advancing, the nourishing, the encouragement, the succouring, the reward of the merit of the individual. Be confident in that belief, for it is individualism without the Tory grub of greed.

What about this problem that some people say they have with the idea of competitiveness? What do they want? An uncompetitive economy? Is anyone going around deliberately looking for a job in an uncompetitive firm? Is anybody trying deliberately to negotiate a bargain in order to bring about uncompetitiveness and the threat to jobs that goes with it. Of course they are not. Don't those who are afraid of accepting the commitment to competitiveness understand that when we make calls – as we all do – for investment in science, in training, in roads and infrastructure, in regions, in education, we are not just demanding the means for social justice, we are also demanding the ingredients of competitiveness? Or are some people so defeatist, so short-sighted, so lacking in conviction that they believe the Tory propaganda that you can only get competitiveness by getting rid of workers, by shutting down firms, by pushing down wages?

Of course, when we make these arguments about individualism and about competitiveness, we make the arguments as the consumers' party – as we always have been from the first day that the first socialist demanded decent health care, decent houses, decent education. They are the basic requirements of consumption because they safeguard basic rights. We do not want those rights buried under bureaucracy or administration. We recognise the fact that all but the most powerful and tenacious individuals are puny when they are faced by an administration, a bureaucracy, a seller much bigger than they in power and stature. That is why we are and always have been, the consumer's party.

When we speak of those things, when we make those arguments about individuals and consumers and competitiveness it is not long before we hear people in the movement saying that we are proposing 'to run the capitalist economy better than the Tories'. Comrades, the day may come when this conference, this movement, is faced with a choice of socialist economies. The debate will be fascinating as the Labour Party conference chooses between the two. But until that day comes, when that choice of socialist economies is actually presented, actually in existence, the fact is that the kind of economy that we will be faced with when we win the election will be a market economy. That is what we have to deal with and we will have to make it work better than the Tories do.

By better, we mean that we combat unemployment, we make the commitment to training, we make the commitment to investment, to paying proper pensions, to funding the National Health Service. Even after that has been the implemented programme of a Labour government for years, there will still be a market, still be a market economy. What will be different will be the condition of the people who have had the chance to train, who will have been engaged in the new industries, who will have benefited not just from the greater production but from the fairer distribution that it finances. That will be applying our values, our vision in practice instead of just talking about it. There is no 'slide to the right' in that. There is no 'concession to Thatcherism' in any of that.

In any case, let me tell this party what so many in this party tell me: the greatest concession to Thatcherism is to let it win again. That is the ultimate concession. Those who are afraid of developing the alternatives that will gain the support of the British people, those who say that they do not want victory at such a price had better ask themselves: if they will not pay that price for winning, what price are they prepared to pay for losing? And who are they prepared to see pay that price? Because I tell you this – the price of defeat is not paid by the people on this platform or even in this hall. The price is paid by the poor. We feel disappointment, frustration, anger when we are beaten. We feel all that. But we will not have to live on poverty pensions. We will not have to go creeping and crawling to the social fund. We will not have to wait in dead end training. We will not have to live on low pay – at least, not most of us here. There are some low-paid workers here paying the price of defeat. Not the rest of us. I am heartily sick of seeing the victims who pay the price of our defeat. I am heartily sick of meeting people in anguish and having nothing to offer them but sympathy and solidarity when I know we should have the power to give them real hope, real support, real backing, real opportunities.

POVERTY IN AFRICA

It is not just here. It is not just those thirteen million people living in poverty in Britain who pay the price. Many more pay the price – women, men and children. There are millions beyond our shores.

This year, Glenys and I went to Zambia, Zimbabwe, Botswana and Mozambique. You might have seen it reported – because the journalists with us were hypnotised by a few minutes of exchange with a very frightened, very nervous soldier in the Zimbabwean army. But that day we had been to Mozambique. That day we had been to two villages in central Mozambique: Chimoio and Inhaminga. Chimoio and Inhaminga are railway villages where the people in their thousands are starving. Not because of floods. Not because of drought. Not because of some dreadful natural catastrophe. They are starving in that village because their village has been isolated by the attacks of the terrorists of RENAMO financed by the South African government.

As Glenys and I got into the square we saw a thousand starving children, not one of them with anything remotely resembling normal clothing. Indeed, Glenys and some of the journalists saw children wearing tree bark, women wearing parachute silk, escaped slaves from RENAMO, women who could testify on the day that they escaped to journalists that the parachute silk had come from ammunition boxes that they had carried from South African sub- marines on a beach in Mozambique. At Chimoio we met an old man in his sixties with his nose and ears clipped off. He had been mutilated because he was the secretary of FRELIMO in his village. And yet we have a Prime Minister who says that sanctions against the state that sponsors the terrorism that commits those atrocities against children and old men and old women would be 'immoral'.

I say to you, when we do not win, it is not just the wretched of our

159

country, the poor and the needy of our country who lose, it is people far away, human beings who need to have in Britain a Labour government committed nationally and internationally to the cause of social justice. Any time anybody is tempted to pass a resolution, to make a statement, to conduct a vote, to hold a demo that a moment's thought would teach them would obscure the true nature, the identity, the effort to gain attention for the policies of the Labour Party, let them pause and think of the people they meet in their Saturday morning surgeries, or the people who might live next door to them, or the kids in Chimoio and Inhaminga who need a government of social justice.

If we remember these things in this movement, out of it will come a solidarity and a unity that makes us an attractive force and a mighty force. It is for those reasons that I listen to the people of our party in their thousands who tell us to get on with compiling the policies that will appeal to the people, that will win us power to apply our principles of social justice and our plans of economic efficiency. I am certain – more certain now than I have ever been – that that is what the people of our party, the people who support our party, the people who want to support our party are looking to us for. Let us do it.

1989
BRIGHTON

'Education and training are now
the commanding heights'

In June 1989, Labour won its first nationwide election since 1974. It won forty-five of Great Britain's seventy-eight seats in the European Parliament; the Conservatives won thirty-two and the Scottish Nationalists one. Labour had also gained the Vale of Glamorgan in a by-election in May.

Labour's recovery in the Spring had two main causes. The first was mid-term Conservative unpopularity, which had been precipitated by economic worries in general and rising interest rates in particular. The second was Labour's successful launch of its second policy review reports, 'Meet the Challenge, Make the Change'. This distanced Labour further than ever before from traditional socialism. The report made clear that the party now gave a low priority to the renationalisation of the utilities privatised by the Conservatives. Any share purchases would be at 'a fair market price'; but there would be few such purchases as money would be tight and a Labour government would not wish to 'pre-empt, for the purposes of transferring ownership, substantial resources which might be applied to other purposes'.

'Meet the Challenge, Make the Change' was a long (80,000 words) and in many places turgid document. Its significance lay in its repeal of some of the party's previous commitments. The largest and most dramatic change concerned defence. Supporters of the existing policy attempted to block the party's adoption of multilateralism. Composite resolution forty-eight asked the conference to 'reaffirm support for policies which unilaterally renounce the use and possession of British nuclear weapons'. This resolution was defeated by 3,635,000 to 2,431,000. The vote, taken twenty-four hours before Kinnock made his speech, finally cremated the cause of unilateralism within the party.

Kinnock invoked eastern Europe's upheaval to justify Labour's new defence policy. Although the Soviet empire did not finally crumble until some weeks after the conference, signs of its imminent collapse were evident. These events were double-edged for the Labour Party. On the one hand they could be proclaimed as a triumph for democratic socialism over the tyrannical variety. On the other hand, there was a danger that the end of communism in country after country would cause socialism of all kinds to be discredited. In the meantime, Kinnock was able to point to the dramas behind the iron curtain and offer them as a reason for new thinking. Thus Labour's new defence policy could be presented not as betrayal of principle but as a considered response to a changing world.

Nobody was fooled by this; but Kinnock did not wish to cause unnecessary offence to many party members who had been unilateralists and had watched with trepidation as Labour's leadership negotiated its U-turn. He did not want to tell them they had been wrong all along, or that their efforts had been worthless; rather he sought to convey the sense that unilateralism had been *right at the time*; now new circumstances demanded new policies. In fact, Labour's switch to multilateralism represented an unambiguous victory for those who had believed that unilateralism had been a wrong-headed policy all along. But Kinnock saw no virtue in demanding an act of collective self-flagellation over Labour's past errors.

Aside from defence, one of Kinnock's tasks in 1989 was to ensure that Labour was not squeezed out of the debate on pollution and the greenhouse effect. In the European Parliament elections, Britain's Green Party had won 15 per cent of the vote. It had not won any seats, but the size of its support startled politicians in all the main parties. The Government responded by stressing the superiority of market forces over state control as a means of protecting the environment; it promised a white paper on new policies in this area. For the second year in succession, Kinnock devoted a large section of his speech to an attack on the Conservatives' record on the environment and an exposition of Labour's alternative.

PK

WE MEET in this conference in a spirit of progress; we meet in a spirit of confidence. The people of Britain know that we have worked for and earned the support that they are now giving to us. They respect us for the changes that we have made and the changes that we are making. Increasingly, they know that we are attuned to the realities of the present and increasingly they are prepared to trust us with the future. People tell me that when I meet them. The polls say that when we read them. But most important of all, we know that we are winning support and understanding and trust because the people tell us when they vote.

They told us that in Pontypridd and the Vale of Glamorgan; they told us that in Vauxhall and in Glasgow Central. They told us that in the county council elections, and all over Britain, in that magnificent victory on 15 June they told us that in the elections for the European Parliament. They keep on telling us – and telling the Labour Party – 'You're doing the right thing. Keep on doing it.' We will keep on doing it. We will keep on because it is the winning way. It is the best way to serve the people we want to stand up for. We will keep on winning. And we will do it with no wheeling, no dealing, no horse-trading and no electoral pacts.

We will put ourselves to the people and we will go on getting their support. We will get it by continuing to construct strong unity of purpose. We will get it by our conduct as a serious, socialist, self-disciplined party. We will go on earning support by having the same candour and confidence that we showed in facing up to ourselves and our times in the policy review. We will get the support by continuing to produce answers that are relevant and practical for the present and for the future, answers that offer the kind of socialism that the people of Britain want. The kind of socialism that insists that the National

Health Service shall not be split up, sold off, privatised, sent to the market, but shall be kept and improved and modernised as a service free of charge at time of need for all the people of this country.

The kind of socialism that the British people understand and support is the kind of socialism that resents the injustice, the cost and the divisiveness of the Poll Tax, that demands a local tax that is fair between people and regions, related to the ability to pay and, for those on low incomes, includes a fair system of rebates to insure against the injustice of tax. The kind of socialism that the British people are attracted by and understand and support is the socialism that takes its inspiration from individual freedom and the right to organise and bargain in freedom collectively. They support that kind of socialism and they resent the centralisation, censorship and control that in the past ten years has given the state more power over the life of the individual in Britain than at any time in modern peacetime history. They do not want that.

The kind of socialism that the people of Britain understand and support is as Tawney described: in the 1930s, in the wake of defeat and division in the Labour Party, he said: 'Socialism is no longer bad politics in Britain unless socialists choose to make it so, which some do with a surprising ingenuity. Nevertheless,' he went on with the right combination of 'a realism that is not torpor and an idealism that is not foolishness,' the Labour Party, a socialist party, is unstoppable because its natural constituency is the majority of the British people. That was true then and it is true now. That is why we are getting the support for the kind of socialism that we are offering to the British people.

THE TORY TEAM

Of course the Tories will try to hit back. They will do it in a variety of ways. First of all, there will be the personal attacks on the Labour leaders. It will not be anything serious – nothing like as serious, for instance, as the personal attacks they make every week of every year on the pensioners, the poor, the homeless and families with children. They are real personal attacks. They really hurt. The next part of the counter-attack will be to order civil servants to waste thousands of hours of time trying to 'cost' our programme. They will push those figures, collected at the taxpayers' expense – such is the nature of the modern Tory state – through the counterfeit machine in Tory Central

Office. You are very familiar with the procedure: it is the one that they have perfected for the purpose of calculating the employment figures, the unemployment figures and Lawson's Budget estimates.

Then there is their secret weapon, the Team. They have got themselves a Team. It was announced last week. Next week, if you should be over eighteen and very stable of mind, put the television on and watch them up at Blackpool. On the back of the stage there will be the slogan 'The Right Team for the Future' – Margaret Thatcher's Team. That is a bit of a confusion in terms, is it not? It is like Dennis Skinner's shyness or David Owen's legions, a real confusion in terms. They have that Team. It is difficult to envisage it really, but since dray horses come in teams, and donkeys and sled dogs come in teams, I suppose the Tories can have a team as well. You can see it now, can you not? The huskies dashing across the icy wastes, eagerly and unquestioningly, with the driver holding a whip over them, saying: 'Mush, mush.' And you know what huskies do, if one of them drops dead don't you? The rest of them eat him. That is the Tory team spirit.

Of course there is a lead dog. The top dog in the team is the Chairman of the Conservative Party, Kenneth Baker. Theirs must be the only political organisation in any democracy in which a move from being in charge of education to being in charge of propaganda is regarded as a promotion. It would not happen anywhere else. He has got that job because he is supposed to be a master strategist. At least that is right. What else could you call a man who presides over education for three years and then, just eight weeks before the country finds out that we are 3,600 teachers short, gets another job? That is a master strategist. He really is a quite brilliant mover. He is the man who invented the Poll Tax and then moved on before it caught up with him.

He was appointed, of course, by the Prime Minister. She is a very considerate person really. There are people who say that she is very remote and detached. I will not have that said about Mrs Thatcher. I have seen her rubbing shoulders with crowds, talking to children, travelling on a train. Pity it was in Japan.

They gave her a lovely reception. They had all the bands out, red carpets. But let's face it: if we had a relationship with a country and they had had a £1 billion trade deficit with us in 1979 and now they had a £5 billion trade deficit with us, I would give them the red carpet treatment. They could have my ticket for the Arms Park. There would be nothing to big.

Japan is a fairly good place to go to listen and to learn. That did not happen when Mrs Thatcher went there. As usual, Mrs Thatcher went there to lecture. She went to instruct the Japanese that if only they would de-regulate, implement free trade policies and remove exchange controls, they too could enjoy the same level of unbounded success as Britain has under Mrs Thatcher. That is what she was telling them. She told them – and she tells us – that we have been enjoying an economic 'miracle'. Nigel Lawson says the same, that we are enjoying a 'miracle', *The Sun*, the *Daily Mail* and even some of the newspapers say the same thing. I suppose it is a miracle of a sort, because if you think about it, when Moses parted the Red Sea and took the children of Israel across, that was a miracle. The trouble was that in the middle of the same miracle along came Pharaoh's army. They got onto the bottom of the Red Sea and it all closed in on them. We have been going through this miracle from the Pharaoh's army eye-view.

But it has been a miracle, truly. We have had oil wealth that none of our major competitor countries has had. At the end of that ten years, Britain has got two million unemployed still – recorded unemployed – the highest inflation rate of any industrialised country, the highest interest rates of any industrialised country, the biggest balance of payments deficit by far of any industrialised country and, to go with it, something that is not too frequently disclosed, a huge net outflow of long term capital. We get lots of money in, because we are offering 14 per cent. It stays for a short time and then moves around, but there is lots going out – incredible for an oil-rich country, but happening under our 'brilliant Chancellor' and our genius business managers. Even with that litany, that is not the worst news. The worst news is that underlying those figures of failures – indeed causing those conditions – is the Tories' refusal, year after year, to make the essential commitment to the productive base of the economy: education and training, research and development, science and the transport and communications system are all objects of gross neglect. We are the only major industrialised country that in the last ten years has continually spent a lower and lower proportion of our gross national product on education; everybody else has been increasing it. Where could be the sense in that?

168

The result of all that was always certain to be an unbalanced economy, under-equipped, under-skilled, inflating and increasingly importing. Britain was bound to become a place of paralysing congestion in some areas, of miserable underdevelopment in others. A place of inefficiency and – yes – because of the neglect of public investment, a place of considerable danger too for the travelling public and for people who work in those industries, as we have seen so tragically demonstrated. That is where they have got us to now.

'WE SHALL INHERIT A MESS'
They have not finished yet. They have still got two years or so to run, which will get us nearly all the way through the time left before the completion of the Single Market of the European Community at the end of 1992. That is going to be a delight, is it not? We shall be part of an open economic zone, operating in a currency exchange rate mechanism in which the pound will be included and subject to even more intensive and direct competition from the other European Community countries than at the present time. And they are countries that all have made and do make a much stronger commitment to skills, research, transport and science than we have under a Tory government. The British government has done absolutely nothing to prepare our country or our people for the challenges or the opportunities of that new Europe. That is the mess they are going to leave to us, because sometime before the completion of the Single Market we shall have a Labour government.

The fact that we shall inherit a mess is nothing really new for us; indeed, every incoming Labour government has inherited a mess from every outgoing Tory government. The only difference is that next time the mess will be even bigger – I say to you soberly, even bigger than the mess has ever been before. No one here or anywhere else should have any doubt about that or the scale of what we shall inherit. No one here or anywhere else should fail to understand that those conditions that we inherit will have the most direct implications for what we do. We are therefore going to have to be very deliberate in our choice of priorities and, having chosen them, we are going to have to stick to those priorities. And we will. Everyone should understand too that if we do anything other than to choose priorities, no matter how tough they are, and stick to them, the result will be that we shall set ourselves the task of doing everything that is desirable and end up doing nothing that is significant.

I do not say that because I am daunted. I do not feel in the least bit defeatist about what I know we shall face, neither do the rest of the people who will form that government, nor indeed the other people in the Parliamentary Labour Party. Nor should you feel daunted; on the contrary. Without any vainglory say that there have been times before when our party has been called in similar circumstances to work for our country in government, generally in dreadful circumstances, circumstances that would have torn a Tory government apart and retarded Britain even further. There are various versions of the history of the Labour Party in government. None of them records any Labour government or any Labour minister as being perfect. But what I would say is that they were patriotic and did their damnedest for their country in a way that no single Tory Cabinet Minister in the bunch that we have got now would think of doing. I do not say any of that about what we shall inherit because I am intimidated by the prospect. I tell you and the British people that because it is the truth.

There is another truth too. There is no easy mechanism, no single, solve-all strategy that can catapult Britain to economic strength. That has been Nigel Lawson's fad over the years, even though he has changed his single instrument once or twice. Success has got to be worked for and it has to be built. That is why we are going to start to do what the Tories should have been doing in these oil-rich years. We are going to start to combat the transport congestion and make the investment in communications without which Britain will judder to an expensive and dangerous halt in a very few years. We will get on with that job. We are going to build up the commitment to science, because if we carry on like we are under the Tories, Britain will be pushed down into the second or third division of the industrial nations. We are going to develop inducements and encouragements for a major expansion of research and development in both the public and private sector, because if we are going to rival our major competitors, we have got a long way to go in catching up with them.

Most important of all, we have got to increase the quality and quantity of skills training and make a new commitment to education in this country. The reason for that is very simple. Now and for all time in the future, human skills and human talents will be the major determinants of success or failure, not just for individuals, but for the

170

whole society in all its social, cultural and commercial life. Education and training are now the commanding heights of every modern economy. We must mobilise all of the available abilities – and I mean all.

In the future which we envisage, therefore, there can be no question of allowing disadvantages in opportunity and access to be suffered by women. We need an economy of all the talents. To get that, we are going to have to make provision to ensure that, for the very best reasons of social justice and economic efficiency, equal rights of education and training are guaranteed and the opportunities are made genuinely accessible by providing support, especially for mothers with children, so that they can enjoy those equal rights in reality.

Comrades, research and development, transport and communications, science, education and training are our priorities. They are the productive base of our economy; they are fundamental to success in the future. If we are to combat inflation, if we are to turn that balance of payments deficit into surplus, if we are to bring down unemployment, if we are to generate the wealth properly to fund and pay for the bills of social justice in a modern society, we are going to have to succeed in building up that base. It means giving that task an unparalleled priority. We will do that. That is the attitude that we will take. It is the practical way.

We know it is the practical way, because it is the way that all of our successful competitors have done it. We know that it is the practical way too, because for the last ten years the other way has been tried, the Lawson way. Is that practical? Is it practical to have neglected and underfunded and run down the foundations of modern industrial strength in order to make tax cuts for the top paid in our country? When that culminates in a prodigious balance of payments deficit, is that practical? Is it practical to use the highest interest rates in the industrialised world to try to squeeze consumer demand when at the very same time those very same interest rates are hammering the very productive industries that we are depending upon to try to pay our way in the world? Is that practical?

Everybody knows that as soon as the supports are shifted in any way, the pound will bounce around all over the place, making it virtually impossible for any company, any concern to plan production or to calculate prices with any certainty. What is all that supposed to achieve? Is the interest rate strategy there to buy us some time so that we can restructure British industry? Is it to buy us some time so that we can get some decent training for the youngsters? Is it to buy us some time so that we can negotiate a new deal in Europe? No, it is not for any of those reasons. The only reason we have got the interest rate strategy is because the Tories do not know what else to do. It is as basic as that.

HOMES AND MORTGAGES

What they are hoping for, of course, is that they can get to a few months before the next general election and then take the brakes off, make some tax cuts and try to deceive the people of Britain yet again that things are back on course. It will not work. It will not work for political reasons; it is one con-trick too far. It will not work for economic reasons either. You do not need to be a economist to know why. All you have to do to know why it will not work economically is to have to pay a mortgage. Those monthly bills are certificates of the failure of Lawsonism.

Nigel Lawson does not see it that way. He says people with mortgages may be finding 'a little difficulty', but that little difficulty, he says, will be 'self-correcting' and we can all look forward to 'a soft landing'. At least he is equipped for that. But if he is in orbit, anticipating a soft landing, nobody else is. If he does not understand the reality of what he has done to people's mortgage payments, he should ask his erstwhile chum, the man who was Chief of Staff at the Tory Central Office in the 1987 election. He was writing in the *Evening Standard* last week. 'Home owners feel cheated', he said. 'Today, they are paying more and more in mortgage repayments for houses that are worth less and less in the market. And those needing to move home too often have to make a marriage-wrenching gamble as the housing market becomes as slippery and dangerous as Brands Hatch on a wet Saturday afternoon.' That is Tory property-owning democracy 1989.

These home-buyers are not the only victims of course. Thousands of elderly people were pleased when this government said they wanted them to make extra provision for their retirement. They liked that idea. But the government did not tell them they were going to slash Housing Benefit, and they did not tell them that in order to make provision for their retirement many of them were going to have either to mortgage or sell the houses that they had spent a lifetime paying for. The greatest victims of the Tories' big cheat in housing of course are those who are suffering because of the gigantic cuts made in house building and who are now in overcrowded accommodation or, in increasing numbers, homeless.

The reason for all that, obviously, is that the Tories never really had a policy for homes; they only ever had a policy for property. It is not the same thing. The Tories never really had a policy for building and renovating or for providing people with real choice between buying or renting. They only ever had a policy really for selling. In this party, we want people to be able to buy houses. That is very important. We want them to be able to buy the houses they previously rented, either in the public sector or the private sector, if that is what they want to do. But what is essential is that they should be able to afford the homes that they buy or rent, and it is essential that if they do not want to buy a house or cannot buy a house, they should still have a residence that they are proud to call home.

There are very few things quite as reassuring and quite as secure as a home, bought or rented, that you know is safe and you know you can afford. There are very few things more intimidating and frightening than having the responsibility of a home that is not safe and that you cannot afford. People are going through agony in Britain now, people who eighteen months or two years ago thought that they were secure and making their way, but have been hit, almost as if they were being assassinated, by the Tory interest rate strategy. That is Tory property-owning democracy 1989.

In this party we have got a housing policy, a real housing policy. One that provides for buying and for renting, building and renovating. One that insists not only on quantity but on quality. One that protects consumers whether they are buyers or tenants in the private or the public sector. And it is a housing policy that is capable of meeting the needs of the future. That is the policy that we offer to the British people, and we offer it in place of the deceit and double- dealing that made so many people feel that they had been cheated by the Tories.

PRIVATISATION

Of course, double-dealing is their stock-in-trade on any number of subjects. I saw a fellow in Risca in my constituency a fortnight ago. He was very exercised about something I will not go into at the present time. 'Tories?', he said, 'Tories are the kind of people who start off promising you the earth and end up selling you water.' That is not a bad definition. They are not only trying to sell it; they are advertising it to you at your own expense. I think that is pretty rich. Do you know why they are having to advertise it and push it so hard? It is because nobody can understand why anybody should want to sell it, so they are having to flog and push and advertise.

Water adverts and electricity adverts – I ask you. 'Electricity is a good thing for you.' I did not know that before. How did I miss out and not realise that water was good for me? A fellow in my office had his prospectus a fortnight ago from the Anglia Water Board. They said, 'As a water user, we are giving you priority.' When I see those adverts on the hoardings and the television, do you know what I am reminded of? Have you ever been in a town in the Soviet Union, especially a big town with those great boulevards? They have those huge, heroic hoardings with preposterous slogans, and paintings of people with muscles on their muscles. You know the ones I mean. They have taken those down in Russia. They are putting them up in Britain. They are putting them up for water and electricity, and I guess we shall go on seeing water ads. It has nothing to do with privatisation, you understand. It is just a coincidence, because a couple of months before water privatisation the regional boards decided that they needed to engage in some public relations. It was a total coincidence; they did not even know there was going to be water privatisation. So we'll continue to see these water ads. But I do not know how much we shall see of the electricity ads, for a few months in any case, because they have got into a total shambles with the effort to sell of electricity. A bigger shambles would only come if they actually managed to sell it off. Comrades, there is a race against time. It is a race between the sale of electricity and the next Labour government.

Indeed, it is a race between not only the privatisation of electricity, but the privatisation of the coal industry as well. Perhaps if they ever really do get around to putting together a Bill, the Privatisation of the Coal Industry Bill, they will at least have the honesty to put an accurate title on it, 'The Termination of the Coal Industry Bill', for that is certainly what it would be.

Shambles or not, they are desperate to sell both water and electricity, not because they want to serve any sensible purpose of the economy or energy, the environment or any strategic purpose. On the contrary, selling either or both of those utilities contradicts every strategic, environmental, logical, industrial and reasonable purpose.

The reason that the government is so anxiously obsessed with selling off these two industries is that they want the receipts so that they can bankroll themselves for the next general election. That is the real reason why they want to sell off electricity and water.

They might succeed in getting under the wire before the election. They might succeed in doing that, but, frankly, it is not going to help them very much at the ballot box, because there are huge majorities in every opinion poll against the sell-off of water and electricity. The reasons are simple. The British people are opposed to the sell-offs because they are more socially responsible, more community minded, more realistic, more far-sighted and more patriotic than the government that governs them. That is why they are against the sell-off of water and electricity.

The people know, as we know, that it is simply wrong to put vital utilities of this kind into the hands of private monopolies, not least because we know – and the British people know – that the whole thrust of privatisation collides head on with environmental concern. Privatisation of water and electricity also puts a great big gaping hole straight through the government's claim to be guardians of the environment. This government cannot prove green credentials simply by moving Nick Ridley – I am not saying anything about the disposal of toxic waste – and replacing him with a much better public relations merchant, Chris Patten, the slick following the Nick. That does not prove green credentials. They do not prove green credentials even by introducing a Green Bill over a year after we offered to draft one for them. For the Tories to have any credibility at all as trustees of the environment, they are going to have to take a much bigger and more serious step. For them to have that credibility, they are going to have to change the whole basis of their philosophy.

The central canon of Thatcherism is that the market is sovereign and that the earth and all that is therein should be governed by the magical movement of demand and supply. Whatever else you can look after with that system, you cannot look after the environment with such a system. This essence of Thatcherism is dressed up as the Big Idea. The reality is that it is a very small, very cheap, very nasty idea. It is an old idea as well. Municipal Tories like Joe Chamberlain rejected it 100 years ago. They rejected it because they said that private monopoly ownership of utilities like water and gas were incompatible with the public good. They knew that 100 years ago, when enterprise capitalism in Britain was red in tooth and claw, a period when Margaret Thatcher would have regarded it as bliss to be alive. But she would not have got a Tory mandate then for water privatisation.

A CLEANER ENVIRONMENT

Market sovereignty of the kind that Margaret Thatcher preaches is most certainly incompatible with the investment in research, the effective regulation, inspection, supervision, prevention, co-operation and decentralisation of powers that are among the essential ingredients of a competent policy for the conservation and improvement of the local, national and global environment. We understand the need to implement such comprehensive policies, and there are working examples to instruct us on many of the most salient objectives.

In Denmark and Sweden two weeks ago I saw how the problem of refuse and the problem of heating homes were brought together to make a solution. Two problems making one solution. In Copenhagen, for instance, the city's refuse is incinerated in conditions which are subject to the most rigorously enforced and constantly improving environmental standards. The resulting heat combines with surplus heat from the city's other power stations to warm 250,000 homes very cheaply and dependably. They have reduced by 30 per cent the energy needed to heat Copenhagen's homes over the past ten years. The residue of the waste is 6 per cent of its original volume. That is a good deal. In a country like ours, where we have a huge amount of waste, some of it lethal and all of it ugly, we know we just cannot keep on piling it up. To serve the future properly we have got to adopt policies that are socially and economically functional and environmentally progressive. The innovations of the Swedes, the Danes and the Norwegians instruct us, and we shall be emulating and improving upon the developments that they have made.

Those innovations go much wider than waste incineration. In the same visit I saw Volvo and SKF, the biggest ball-bearing manufacturer in the world – two companies as hard-nosed and competitive as any companies anywhere – implementing the environment policies worked out in conjunction with the government, local authorities, environmental groups and trade unions. Those companies are prospering, not in spite of the environmental conditions which they satisfy, but because of those conditions. That was the testimony of the companies. They acknowledge that the stimulus comes from the government that sets environmental targets and timetables to achieve them. The same companies told me that they bettered the targets and the timetables; they had reduced their waste and attained greater efficiency in the process, reducing marginal costs. They do not regard such government involvement as 'interfering'. In this and many other ways they consider government involvement to be normal and necessary.

I am not describing perfection. I do not have the awe of a return visitor from an environmental Shangri La. I am not saying that what they have got is perfect; they would not accept that it was and certainly it is not. I am saying that in this country we could – and we must – make such progress in exactly the same way. In government we are determined to achieve that, and even in the couple of years before we are elected, we are going to use the evidence of those working models to campaign for the speediest possible change in our country, which is getting dirtier and more dangerous by the minute.

There are some of course who believe that concern for the environment is largely a passing anxiety of the affluent who have nothing else to worry about. That is wrong on all counts. The concern is not passing. The concern is here to stay, and the only change will be that it will get bigger. Anybody who believes that the concern stops with the well-heeled has only to go to some of Britain's cities, where in the Thatcher years the rat population has grown substantially, not out of sympathy with the Conservative party, but because of changed eating habits and because of sewers that are in increasing disrepair, through no fault of the local authorities. In those and other areas, damp and disrepair are the greatest environmental concerns. A fellow said to me not very long ago, at the beginning of the summer before it really started to get warm, that he had terrible damp problems. It was just at the time that they started advertising water. He said: 'Be an H2Owner? I thought I had a monopoly – it's coming out of my walls.' The environmental concern runs right through all levels of society.

It goes a great deal further than the people who are far from affluent in our towns and cities. The poorest people in the world are the most environmentally concerned. For them the problems of the environment are not questions relating to the welfare of the ozone layer in ten or twenty years' time. The problems of the environment for them relate to their immediate and fragile conditions. For them, the condition of the environment is a matter of eating or not eating, living or not living. They are the wretched of the earth. They are the most environmentally concerned.

But as they try to care – and very often succeed – for the land that they farm and graze, the pressures of poverty are such that very often they are fighting a losing battle. That will go on unless we in this far and prosperous North of the world do much more to help them beat their poverty. But instead of giving help on the scale that is needed, the industrialised nations, the IMF and the World Bank operate finance and debt strategies which have done the opposite of giving help. They have ensured a huge flow of wealth from the poor countries to the rich countries; and the banks have been the major beneficiaries. Between 1983 and 1987, aid payments to countries in Sub-Saharan African totalled $58 billion. In the same period $45 billion came out in debt payments. The situation in Latin America is even more stark. Between 1983 and 1987, countries of Latin America received about $28 billion in aid and paid out $226 billion in bank loan repayments. That cannot be right.

Far from easing the pressure on the people and on the land, the industrialised countries are intensifying the pressure. It is a terrible global injustice, but it is shocking global stupidity too. In the very act of burdening the people and land of the developing countries with huge payments, the financiers and governments are burdening their own people and their own lands too. Environmental degradation is a communicable disease. Even the most short-sighted in the Northern hemisphere must realise that if we do not help the poor countries to be green and pleasant, we will not have green and pleasant lands ourselves anywhere in the world.

As part of the strategy for trying to safeguard the future therefore those debts must be radically and rapidly reduced and, as frequently as is possible, cancelled. Development aid must go directly to the poor who know best how to use it. They are the most skilled guardians of the earth, if they are ever given a chance. Developed countries, and the people in developed countries, must adopt fair price regimes so that the people of the poor countries have the breathing space and the income to enable them to protect and improve their environment, both for their own sakes and, yes, for our sakes too.

That is what we put in the policy review. It is an argument for global citizenship, a recognition of the fact that in the world now and for all the future, passive co-existence is not enough; active co-operation to defeat common problems is essential to environmental security for every country. It is essential for every other form of security too.

THE BREAK-UP OF EASTERN EUROPE

It is certainly vital in the changing relationship between East and West. We are now at the beginning of the time when we can, in George Bush's words when he visited Germany earlier this year, 'open up the possibilities' for Europe to forgo the peace of tension for the peace of trust. Even in the few months since he said that, Poland and Hungary have had their first free elections in many decades. The televised proceedings of the People's Congress of Deputies in Moscow has shown us the extraordinary and encouraging sight of democratic arguments in that body.

This very day in East Germany, on the anniversary of the establishment of the German Democratic Republic, people are demonstrating in their thousands on the streets for freedom. When all that is happening, we know that Europe – the whole of this continent – is never going to be the same again. As Mikhail Gorbachev said in the United Nations last December: 'There's no going back for anyone'. That is now a central truth of the age; indeed it is a central hope of the age. A momentum is well under way, and whilst there can be no accurate estimate of its speed, the direction is certain. In this party we want to be part of that progress, part of that momentum, making the changes, taking the opportunities. We seek the power to do that. To stop being spectators and start being negotiators. To take our country off the sidelines and put it in the mainstream of advance, where it should rightly be, exercising its influence for understanding improved world relationships. That is what we will do.

In the still deep divisions of ideology between East and West there are of course suspicions and rivalries built up over more than seventy years, which are not going to vanish in a year, or in five years or maybe even in ten years. Because of that, security will continue to mean armed security. But it must also increasingly mean – and it does increasingly mean – the security of negotiated disarmament and the security of developing social and economic relationships. In other countries of the NATO alliance that is not only understood, it is being pursued with a vigour which is absent from the British Government.

There are other members of NATO – notably West Germany – who are already operating agreements to train thousands of young Russians to broaden the business relationships, to offer new technologies. A new dual-track towards security is being built, not a bit like the old one. On it, the efforts for negotiated disarmament are running alongside increasing economic engagement.

We want to travel that track. We want to do it for our own interests of security and stability and economic prosperity. We also want to do it because we know that the pressure for freedom that is exercising its irresistible force among the people of the Eastern Bloc needs to be reinforced by economic support from democracies. For the danger will be that if the new liberty being experienced in the trail-blazing countries like Poland and Hungary is surrounded by poverty and under-development in the early years, then that liberty will be fragile. Even the sweet taste of the freedom that these people have yearned for can turn sour if it does not bring with it the beginning of material advancement. Those countries therefore have to make the leap from the command economy to the market economy, from the single party state to pluralism. The problem is that it is physically impossible for them – and physically impossible for anybody – to leap slowly. It is essential therefore that the West – and especially the European Community countries – give support to try to ensure that the take-off of those emerging democracies is firm and their landing is certain and stable.

I have talked to democratic socialists from Poland. They explained to me that it is totally understandable that people in large numbers want to make the lurch directly from what they have known, with its shortages and its queues and its inadequacies, to what they believe to be the free market society, as advertised in the glossy magazines. Those who have been exiles in the West, good comrades in the democratic socialist exiled parties, some of whom have gone back to their own countries for the first time in thirty or forty years and others much younger, tell us that their main task is to counsel people that the best path in those countries is not at either end of the pendulum, but actually in employing the mixture of necessary regulation and the dynamic of the market. The only political philosophy that really offers the opportunity to do that is the democratic socialism that they have been seeking to uphold in those countries all those years. I think that is a tribute to the scope and energy of democratic socialism. And as people think about it the logic is bound to appeal.

In the meantime, before people come to final decisions, when this maelstrom of new liberty is swirling in those countries what we have got to do is to provide the maximum opportunity and the best support that we can offer to ensure that people do not just get their freedom, but get the chance to build their standard of living as well. Our country should already be properly involved in that support, certainly in the form of technical and training aid. But once again we see the ambivalent Prime Minister making gestures of encouragement and simultaneously using the language of tension. A couple of weeks ago, when she was in Japan, she described these changes in the Eastern Bloc with their great and inspiring possibilities, for the advance of liberty as 'a period of uncertainty and danger'. It need be neither. Of course, no one is asking that defences be utterly dismantled in celebration of the election of Solidarnosc to government. I have not heard anybody advocating that. On the contrary, there could be a period of greater certainty and greater safety if people like Mrs Thatcher really wanted the advance of those conditions and were prepared not just to talk about it, but to do something about it. But yet again, even at this time of great opportunity to use democracy, to help democracy, we see Mrs Thatcher holding back.

It is always the same. From East-West disarmament negotiations to the attitude they adopt in the Commonwealth towards South Africa, to international environmental co-operation, relationships with the Third World and their posture within the European Community, Margaret Thatcher shows that she is from the Greta Garbo school of diplomacy, 'I want to be alone'. That is the constant theme. It is not splendid isolation or cunning or sagacity or diplomatic skin. It is a fundamental failure to perceive and to try to secure Britain's role in a rapidly changing Europe and a rapidly changing world. She is out of touch, out of date and out of step with the British people.

We are in step. We share the British people's recognition of the reality that we have got a positive part to play in the development of the new relationship between East and West. We share their recognition, as they demonstrated it on 15 June, of the reality that we have got an essential part to play in a European Community that belongs at least as much to us as it belongs to anybody else. We are going to make it work in a way that can simultaneously develop it as a community and not just as a market. We are going to see that our country is safeguarded and stimulated and not emptied by that pull to the centre – a movement from Britain and other countries in the Community that would be devastating for so much of the European Community.

CONCLUSION

We will do that job properly, because you see, comrades, what these issues and many like them demonstrate is one of the biggest differences between the Tories and ourselves. In every sphere of policy, international and domestic, the big difference is that we are going forward to face the future to meet it, to try to shape it in the best interests of the British people. The Tories are just waiting for the future to hit them. That is all that can explain the way in which they are so confused over these great changes going on in the world. The way indeed in which, even knowing the fixed date of the arrival of the completion of the Single Market, they made no preparation for it; they just waited for it to come and wash over them. They made no preparation for the Channel Tunnel. They are supposed to be the great sponsors of that idea. They consulted no one, neither locally nor nationally. They did not plan, they did not invest. They will not finance the railways; they do not even know the regions exist. Now they do not even know if they can finance the finishing of the Tunnel. When people are so purblind, when people are so incapable even of working towards fixed targets of the future, when they do not have to guess, look into crystal balls or make estimates, but have got a precise date and still mess it up, there is no part of the future that they are fit to rule.

That attitude towards tomorrow that they have is not good enough to serve the future. They are not good enough for the British people. We are now. I know that, you know that. You feel, you rejoice in and you work to increase the support that we have got. It is not an empty claim to say that this Conference is one of progress, is one indeed of celebration, not one of relaxation or of complacency. In Robert Frost's words, we have 'miles to go' and 'promises to keep'. That should always be a guide for socialism. There is no time in socialism anywhere at all where we can take it easy, lean back, say the job is done. Nobody here will say that. But it is an encouragement, an inspiration to see this party working together, coming to a joint position on objectives, and not only telling itself, but exuding to the British public the feeling that we are fit to serve our country.

As I think of those things, I would like to put my feelings into words greater than anything I could ever produce, the words of Percy Bysshe Shelley:

'A brighter dawn awaits the human day.
When poverty and privilege,
The fear of infamy
Disease and woe,
War with its million horrors and fierce hell shall live,
But only in the memory of time.'

Let us seek power. Let us earn power. Let us be elected to power. Let us use power to ensure that all of those evils are put into the memory of time and we shall greet the brighter dawn of that day.

1990
BLACKPOOL

'We need an active partnership with
the private sector'

For once, the dominant concerns at Labour's 1990 conference were the Government's troubles rather than Labour's own problems. Margaret Thatcher's government had had a terrible year. The introduction of the poll tax in April 1990 had propelled Labour briefly to an opinion poll lead of more than twenty points. Gallup's March survey had found Thatcher to be the least popular Prime Minister since records began. Mortgage rates were at record levels. Inflation had climbed to 10 per cent. And by the autumn of 1990 the economy was moving into recession.

These difficulties were compounded by a series of cabinet disputes over the Government's European policies. Thatcher had lost two cabinet ministers over this issue during the previous twelve months – Nigel Lawson, her Chancellor of the Exchequer, and Nicholas Ridley, her Trade and Industry Secretary. As Labour met, doubt still persisted on whether Britain would join the exchange rate mechanism of the European Monetary System. In the event, the decision to join was announced just hours after the Labour conference ended, on Friday 5 October.

Even further into the future – though not far – lay Sir Geoffrey Howe's resignation, which sparked the chain of events that culminated in Thatcher's replacement as Prime Minister by John Major. For the time being, Labour could meet in conference with the warm glow of watching their rivals on the run – a reverse of the pattern of party conferences through much of the 1980s.

Internationally, two events dominated the months preceding Labour's conference: the collapse of the Soviet empire in eastern Europe (Kinnock made his speech on the day East Germany ceased to exist as a separate country); and Iraq's invasion of Kuwait.

From the moment that Kuwait was invaded in August, Kinnock

had given unambiguous backing to the Government, and to Thatcher personally, for the way they handled the crisis. It was a measure of Kinnock's authority within his party that his stand was opposed by relatively few Labour MPs or activists. In common with other international crises, Kinnock knew that the Kuwait invasion would help the Government in the short run: but badly-judged opposition tactics might intensify that effect. In 1982 Labour had reacted to Argentina's invasion of the Falkland Islands far less decisively than the Government, and the party had paid a price for its vacillation. Kinnock ensured that Labour did not repeat that mistake on this occasion. By the time Labour gathered at Blackpool, Kinnock had spoken twice at length in support of the Government – in a special debate in the House of Commons, and at the Trades Union Congress. His reference to the invasion in his conference speech amounted to a brief restatement of his position, rather than a major new announcement of party policy.

Labour's domestic policies were refined rather than changed in 1990. The major issues – concerning markets, the role of the state, nationalisation and, above all, defence – had been largely settled by 1989. The policy content of Kinnock's speech was therefore directed more at consolidation, and tackling three important fears that had been raised about Labour's programme for government.

The first fear was that a Labour government would wreck the economy, forcing taxes and interest rates to rise. In his speech, Kinnock countered this by arguing for a package of policies including membership of the ERM and lower interest rates. (On both points he anticipated Government policy by precisely three days.) On taxation, Kinnock was more cautious. He had previously told television interviewers that there would be no increase for the majority of standard rate taxpayers: on this occasion he stated that there should be no income tax *cuts* 'for many years to come', as the money was needed instead for health, welfare, education and the environment.

The second fear was that a Labour government could not work effectively with private industry. In this speech, Kinnock presented himself as a friend of industry; he said that Labour would adapt the policies of other countries where government and industry worked in partnership.

The third fear came more from inside his own party than outside – that Labour's policies had become so consensual that the party had no 'big idea': its radicalism had disappeared; the fire in its belly had been extinguished. Kinnock attempted to counter this by making the need for better education and training the core of his speech for the second year in succession. But here, as with other policies, Kinnock was severely constrained by the party's commitment – in the words of John Smith, his shadow Chancellor, the day before – that 'we will not spend more than the economy can afford'. So while Kinnock attacked the Tories for reducing the share of national income being spent on education, he was unable to offer a timetable for making up the shortfall.

In this, as in other ways, Kinnock's need to demonstrate financial rectitude overrode his ambitions to spend more on public services. This posed the danger that he would end up satisfying nobody – as he might be seen as cautious by those who wanted greater radicalism, but as secretly spendthrift by those who favoured caution. Kinnock's 1990 speech was an attempt to persuade a sceptical electorate that Labour would be competent in government, and that responsibility and radicalism could sit comfortably together.

PK

WE MEET in this conference in strength and in the confidence that progress and advance bring to us. When we met last year we had over 8,600 Labour councillors in Britain and had control in 164 councils. That was a record. Now, this year, we have well over 8,900 councillors in Britain and control of a higher record of 175 councils. When we met last year Mid-Staffordshire was a Conservative parliamentary seat with a Tory majority of 14,000. Now it is a Labour seat with a majority of 9,000.

When we met last year, you will remember that the Tory Party was loudly proclaiming that they had what they called 'the right team for the future'. You will remember Kenneth – not Kenneth Branagh, but Kenneth Baker – playing Prince Hal: 'He which hath no stomach to this fight, let him depart'. Three weeks later Nigel Lawson went. Two months later Norman Fowler went. Three months later Peter Walker went, and then two months after that off went Nicholas Ridley, kaput, as they say. They were billed as 'the right team for the future.' Comrades, I have seen the future and it has nearly all resigned.

Much else of course has changed in this last year, not all for the better. A year ago at their annual conference the Tories were promising that they would make the economy stonger. It is now in recession. They promised to get inflation down. Then it was 7.4 per cent; now it is 10.6 per cent. They promised to get interest rates down, and on the Thursday of their conference interest rates went up from 14 per cent to 15 per cent. It has been a further year of Tory failure.

But the real problem is not just that things are worse now than they were last year. The real problem is that in so many vital respects things are worse now than they were eleven long years ago. When Mrs Thatcher became Prime Minister in 1979, Britain, like every other country, was suffering the effects of major increases in oil prices.

190

Britain's inflation was too high: it was at the European Community average. Now, after eleven years, it is nearly double the European Community average. In 1979, unemployment was 1.25 million and falling; now it is 1.6 million, even by the new accounting system, and rising. Then – eleven years ago – the balance of payments was roughly in balance; now we are heading for a £17 billion deficit this year, following a £20 billion deficit last year, following a £15 billion deficit the year before. They are definitely going for the Triple Crown this year: three deficits above £10 billion. In terms of inflation, unemployment, balance of payments, economic growth, interest rates, manufacturing investment, housing starts, tax burden, world trade share, domestic trade share and so many other measures of performance, the Tories are not even back at square one after eleven years.

Confronted by all of that, Mrs Thatcher could only say, with a sob in her voice, when she was interviewed last week by a newspaper, that it was likely that no income tax cuts could be made next year 'because of the Gulf crisis'. Even by her standards that was a pretty lame excuse. No one believes that the current economic nose-dive began with the invasion of Kuwait. Everyone knows that it is the direct result of Tory policies that long pre-date the aggression of Saddam Hussein. But in any case, whatever desperate excuse the Prime Minister thinks up for not cutting income tax, I have to say that I do not think that income taxes should be cut next year. I think that the children and the pensioners and the sick people of Britain come a long way before income tax cuts next year or for many years to come.

Of course tax bands can be changed to increase fairness, savings and investment can be encouraged through the tax system to increase efficiency, and there is one tax that can be cut – the poll tax. We are going to cut it out of existence altogether. The Tory idea that general cuts in income can be justified in a country where the schools are underfunded, the wards are being closed, the land, the water and the air are dirty and the streets are not safe is rejected not only by me, but by the great majority of the British people. Such ideas deserve to be rejected, not because no one likes to pay tax, but because anyone with any sense at all knows that further general reductions in income taxation mean further general decline in the standards of provision that are essential to life in a civilised, secure community.

If the Tories cannot cut income tax, what are they going to do? They have only ever got one answer to that: 'Keep interest rates up, keep on squeezing the economy, keep on the pressures of recession and eventually,' they say, 'inflation will come down and all will be well.' That is their plan. It will not work; it never works. Kenneth Baker said as much last week: 'We've dealt with inflation twice before,' he said. That rather begs the question, doesn't it? If you have dealt with inflation twice, why have you got to do it three times? If they dealt with inflation in 1980, why did it come back in 1985? If they dealt with it in 1985, why is it back now? The answer is that they did not 'deal with' inflation. Their single response of very high interest rates can of course bring the inflationary temperature down. It can cool the fever. But high interest rates cannot by themselves combat the virus of inflation. On the contrary, high interest rates inflict such wounds on the economy that the higher investment costs, the higher production and living costs that they leave behind, even after the rates have been temporarily cut, make the economy yet more prone to weakness and the return of inflation. That has happened twice in the last Tory decade. That is what will happen again unless they radically change their policies. Sadly, there is not too much of a chance of that.

So what should they be doing now in the circumstances that they have created by their own incompetence and irresponsibility? I will tell them, not from some academic sideline or as the leader of a minority party with no prospect of power or even years away from a general election where events may intervene. I will tell them what they should do to help our country now, and do it from the standpoint of someone who knows that within the next twelve or eighteen months, whenever the Tories choose to call a general election, we shall win that election and face the problems, the legacy and the mess that they leave.

What should they do? First, they should cut the very high interest rates and so reduce industrial and housing costs. That is what we would do. That is what we will do if interest rates are at their current level. Secondly and simultaneously, in order not to release a consumer credit spree that would suck in imports, they should introduce controls on the supply of credit, restraints in what the banking system is allowed to lend. Several other mixed economies do it successfully. That is what we would do. That is what we will do.

Thirdly, they should be negotiating entry into the exchange rate mechanism of the European Monetary System, not as a short term anti-inflationary measure, a wing and a prayer, not as an electoral expedient, which is how they now see it, but as a strategic means of providing stability to the British economy and to British producers. That is what we would do. That is what we will do: interest rate cuts, credit controls, negotiated entry to the exchange rate mechanism. They are not what the Prime Minister calls 'soft options'. There are no soft options anywhere at any time for anybody. But there are sensible options. They are the changes necessary to bring the beginnings of cost reductions and stability that are vital to the productive economy. They are not easy, but they are certainly better than continuing to squash whole areas of the industrial economy with insupportable interest rates. They are the sensible option. Crushing industry is the suicide option. That is what they are doing.

GOVERNMENT AND INDUSTRY

Of course, when people speak in such terms the Prime Minister describes them as the voices of gloom. She does not like that. So, ever the gentleman, permit me to be the voice of optimism. Let me set aside the gloom and say that in this country of ours there is enterprise and innovation; there is initiative. There are many managements and workforces with shared objectives. There are great skills of design and adaptation. There is a widespread desire to compete effectively, because everybody knows that ultimately their prosperity and security depend upon it, and when companies and workforces call for change in the government's economic policies, they are not engaging in special pleading, they do not want featherbedding; all they want is a context in which they can properly prove themselves. That context, that environment for success, is simply not being provided by a government that hits them with very high interest rates 60 to 70 per cent above those that have to be paid by their competitors in the same trade. It is not being provided by a government that refuses to make the commitment to research and training that is common amongst our competitors.

Even as I describe the conditions that disadvantage our producers, as they are very frequently put to me by people on both sides of industry, I can already hear the Tories saying: 'These aren't the responsibilities of government. Industries should stand on their own feet. All these matters should be left to the market.' That is the constant mantra of the last eleven years. Other governments do not think like that. Even if in public they say they think like that, in private they certainly do not act like that. When governments in

Japan, France, Germany and other countries provide the long term support to industry and ours does not, it really is no good for the Prime Minister, the Chancellor of the Exchequer or Nicholas Ridley to cry: 'Foul'. They have to understand that we are not involved in cricket but in ruthless competition, and they have to give our people a fair chance, as other countries give their people a fair chance.

That competition is hotting up. Just twenty-seven months from now the European Community will be a completed single market. If the government here does not do what must be done to help to strengthen the performance of British industry, inflation will remain a recurrent plague and the slide into deficit and debt, unemployment and insecurity will continue. It is to stop that slide, to provide the realistic alternative, that our Labour policies give the highest possible priority to the long term measures that will increase productive and competitive strength in Britain. Nothing supersedes that.

We have got to employ science. We have got to mobilise the skills of women and men on equal terms. We have got to modernise our transport system and diffuse new technologies throughout industry. Above all, we have got to raise the standards of training and education to levels that at least compare with those of our main competitors. So much is obvious; yet ours is the only major industrial country which is spending less on research and development as a share of national wealth than it did ten years ago. The under-funding of research and development, the shortage of qualified science teachers in our schools, the brain-drain of scientists and technologists to other countries, the crisis of morale that is reported from so many parts of the science community, are not isolated features. They are the results of a bias against science, the disregard of the importance of research and development, the refusal to invest in ideas in an age when that investment is critical to any possibility of success. That attitude must be reversed. We will do that.

We will shift spending from military to civil research and development in order to get better economic value for public investment. We will increase basic research, bring it together with industrial needs and achieve the successful technology transfer that is increasingly common in the economies of our competitors. Like those competitors, we will provide security and continuity in research and development by using takeover regulations and tax policies to see that firms that are making the research and development commitment are

194

not targeted by takeover predators, which too often is the case. With those and other changes we will be developing a long term infrastructure for science in Britain.

We need to do the same with transport. Amongst the most vital components of the modern, integrated transport system that Britain needs to succeed there must be modern, high speed rail links running from Scotland and Wales through the length and breadth of England to the Channel tunnel and on to the European mainland beyond. We will build those rail links. We will do it through a financial partnership between public and private sectors. That is how the TGV has been financed in France, and now, ten years after it was embarked upon, the TGV network is not only spreading prosperity to the regions of France, stimulating investment and creating jobs, but repaying its capital costs and earning a healthy return for public and private investors alike. That would never have happened without the French socialist government making exactly the long term commitment that the British Tory government over the same period has categorically refused to make. Nothing could more clearly express the great gap in the attitudes between a government that has an active partnership with the private sector in strengthening the economy and a government whose perverse ideology will not allow such a productive relationship.

Every commuter, every driver, every business – and therefore every citizen in Britain – is paying dearly for that dogma. It is inefficient, it is anti-scoial, it neglects the environment, it disables the economy. That dogma is a barrier across the road to national progress. Everyone now knows that the only way to clear away that block is to get rid of the government that forms the block across the road to progress. We will use the combination of public and private funding to the benefit of the public and the private interest in Britain.

EDUCATION IN CRISIS

A strategic policy for science and technology and a modern transport system are essential components of a long term economic strategy. But without doubt the most fundamental requirement of future success is improvement in the British education system. Parents know it. Employers, teachers and students themselves know it. The general public knows it. They also know that there is a crisis in British education. Everybody realises that with the exception of the government. Only the government denies it. They deny it not only because they are completely out of touch with the realities of the state schooling system in our country, but because they are also out of sympathy with the state schooling system that provides for a huge majority of the parents and children of this country.

They have got to be replaced by a government that is in touch, a government committed to improvement, a government of people who do not favour the maintained schools in any abstract sense, but who support them because those schools educate their own children. The only government of that character, as Jack Straw brilliantly demonstrated yesterday, will be the Labour government. The Conservative government's practice of treating schools as if they are laboratories to test out the latest Tory social engineering theories has got to stop. They disrupt, divide and demoralise children, parents, teachers and communities. They do nothing for general standards in results or in conduct. They have little to do with learning and everything to do with political meddling.

In this party and, I believe, in this country people want improved education, not perpetual experimentation with the lives and futures of their children. We regard it, first, to be essential to improve the provision of the equipment of education: the supply of qualified teachers, the essential books and learning materials, the buildings and facilities which are vital ingredients of an up-to-date education system. Teachers, books, materials, buildings – it is called getting back to basics: the basics that will ensure that teachers are able to give more attention to individual children, the basics that foster achievement in reading, writing, numbers – yes, and in cultural and sporting activities, because they too are essential to the rounding and good grounding of every youngster. No youngster should be denied the chance of access to music, literature and sport. None should be denied that; too many are now. The basics include those fundamental requirements of actively encouraging parents to be involved in and informed about the education of their children, partners with the schools instead of being continually regarded as being an alternative source of funding because the government will not provide the resources.

Secondly, as a feature of our approach to education we will get rid of the concept that education for the majority is something that begins round about five and ends round about sixteen. That is why we aim to provide nursery education for every three and four-year-old whose parents wish to exercise that choice. It is vital not only for the advantage of the child and its social and educational development, but for the liberty and the choice of men and women parents who want to sustain careers, who need frequently to get jobs and should not, as was said from this platform yesterday, perpetually face the dilemma of making a choice between a reasonable standard of living and caring in the way that they want to for their children. I have to say that I read in a report this morning that Mrs Thatcher, speaking in the wake of the meeting that she attended of the United Nations this weekend, spoke of the need for mothers to give attention to nurture and provide wisdom. Nobody in their right mind could disagree with that. But I wish the Prime Minister comprehended the advantage – the wonder – of being able to do that with your children and would do something to ensure that many more parents could do it with their children too, because they love their children as much as she ever loved hers. We shall implement our policies to reform education and training after sixteen and provide access to vocational and academic courses through which people can earn qualifications appropriate to their needs and abilities.

Thirdly, the cuts in central government funding for education have got to stop. Huge losses have been inflicted on education in Britain over these years. This year the Tory government will be allocating 4.8 per cent of gross national product to all forms of central expenditure on education. If they had maintained the commitment of the last Labour government – 5.5 per cent of GNP – Britain's primary and secondary schools, colleges, polytechnics, and universities would this year be £3.6 billion better off than they are now. Figures and percentages of GNP are immensely boring. Figures of £3.6 billion are immensely boring. But translate that in terms of teachers, books, decent classrooms, access to university and higher education, and all of a sudden they become immensely exciting, the greatest adventure that people can have, the fulfilment of their own desire to find their education liberation. That is denied when the GNP is cut back on that scale.

No one expects that we shall be able immediately or even in years to make up fully this huge shortfall. We will strive to do it, naturally, but such is the position from which we shall have to start after the years of Toryism that we are going to have to build up to those levels. That is what our neighbours and competitors did. They did not achieve their educational and economic success by borrowing wildly or by taxing fiercely. We shall not be doing either of those. They did it by committing the public expenditure that they could afford and, above all, by keeping on doing it year after year. We must do the same.

I will give you an example of what I mean. France, like every other country, is today under economic pressure as a result of the Gulf crisis. Unlike Britain, they have no oil of their own, and in their budget published a fortnight ago the government has tightened expenditure in many areas in order to cope with the present and projected costs arising from the Gulf emergency. But there is an exception to that budgetary restraint – indeed, there is an exemption. Their education budget has not been reduced at all. Their education budget for this financial year is increased by 9 per cent. That is what you mean when you say that socialism is the religion of priorities, a 9 per cent increase in the education budget, even in straitened circumstances. They have been following those policies for ten years through thick and thin. They have done it because they know that if they want strength, they must have skill, and if they are to have skill, they must have more people educated to a higher level in smaller classes with sufficient teachers. That is the only way in which it adds up. They are not just talking about it or wishing for it, they are getting on with it. They are investing in it.

The French education is obviously not without its blemishes, but what is not in doubt is the superiority of their levels of participation, access and opportunity. Participation, access and opportunity are the keys to unlock the door to achievement – not just economic advance, but cultural and spiritual fulfilment, for that also – indeed mainly – is what education is about too. We are not in the business of seeking to produce a computer age version of hewers of wood and drawers of water. We want capable people, confident people, demanding citizens, people who are adaptable and applicable. Education is the key to giving people all of that opportunity. It has advanced in France. We have got to catch up with that with the next Labour government. We must provide those keys. In education, as in so many other fields, our country can only get out what it puts in. If we want to get out of education the skills of the future for the people of the future, we have to put in now and keep on putting in.

Obviously, it will not be enough to do it only in education. It must be done in training too. The reason for that is obvious. Eight out of ten people who will be in our workforce in the year 2000 are already of working age and they need training for work and in work. Over two-thirds of the working people in Italy, Germany, France and Spain are getting some skilled vocational training. But in Britain, after eleven years of Conservative government, only a little over one-third of our working people get any training at all. That is hardly surprising when the government seems to regard training not as a key to economic success, but as a branch of social security – and a pretty flimsy branch at that. Now, after a decade of de- skilling, the government is cutting more millions from the training budget. When there are no incentives to train, no advice on how to train, no targets for quantity or quality that compare with those of our competitor countries, it is not surprising that so many companies do not make the proper training commitment.

As you heard from Tony Blair yesterday, the Labour government's national training strategy will be used to overcome that great strategic weakness. It will be built on a practical national and local partnership between employers, trade unions and the providers and users of education and training. We will concentrate on the quantity and quality of training and qualifications from training that will be adaptable in the service of women and men throughout their working lives in order to meet and master the changes that they will encounter with great rapidity. That is why we shall be giving strong encouragement to the industries and employers who do make a proper commitment to training. It is also the reason why we shall require employers who do not train, but who 'pirate' from the responsible firms, either to change their ways or to make a financial contribution so that training can be provided.

At the level of the national economy, the industry, the firm and the individual, we shall be working to enable Britain to become a capable country. We shall do it not only to ensure that individuals have greater control over their lives and their futures, but also because we know that in the 1990s the technological revolution and the advance of our country's fortunes depends upon success in the training revolution.

HEALTH AND COMMUNITY CARE
Those policies for the strengthening of Britain's productive and competitive performance have obvious purposes. They are essential if our country is to pay its way. They are essential if our producers are to

generate the wealth necessary for future investment. They are essential too if we are to generate the wealth that is necessary to provide high and rising standards of social justice, welfare support and opportunity in our country. They are policies that will the means, and do not just demand the ends.

That is essential if we want to pay – and keep on paying – proper pensions. It is essential if we want to fund fully – and go on funding fully – the National Health Service. That is what we will do. We will start to do it by bringing the opted-out hospitals back into the NHS. By next April hospitals are supposed to clear their debts and their books to prepare for what the Tories call 'reforms'. Once again we are on the brink of a winter of cuts and closures and distress and pain; but this time it is all being made deliberately worse by a government intent on wrecking the national health service. That is the real price of Tory health care. That is why no one in this country can afford another Tory government.

Certainly, even outside the hospitals and the formal structure of the NHS, there are millions of people, who are chronically ill and being cared for in their own homes, who cannot afford another Tory government. In this country there are six million people looking after others, usually relatives, who are young, long-term sick, disabled, elderly or fragile – six million carers. The overwhelming majority of them are women. The government has praised their selflessness to the skies, dripping with braid, knobs on and bands playing. But only 110,000 out of the six million carers get invalid care allowance. That same praising government has cut carers' benefits. They have forced cuts in carers' services. They have taken away carers' rights to unemployment benefit. This year, to cap it all, the government postponed community care in order to save a few pennies on the poll tax. The government that claims to have produced economic miracles and tries to tell us that the economy has underlying strength broke its pledge to provide the package of nursing and home care, day care and respite care that should have been available through community care. Next week the Tory Party conference will meet under the slogan 'The Strength to Succeed'. I just wonder what sort of strength it takes to inflict blow after blow on people who are trying to care for their desperately sick loved ones in their own homes. I would say it was brutal strength, wouldn't you?

No wonder caring families feel cheated. They are not asking for much help. They are not asking to be relieved of their obligations. They would do what they do in any case in the cause of love and duty. Often they do it in circumstances of dire poverty and isolation, at risk to their own physical and mental health. If these six million people did not do it – or even a large proportion of them – the rest of us would have to find the funds to pay for beds in long stay residential care for elderly people at a cost of over £200 a bed per week. The costs would be vast.

As well as being humane, it makes sense therefore to operate a comprehensive system of community care with earmarked local government funds. It makes sense to develop a carers' benefit, as we are doing. It makes sense to allocate responsibility for this major part of the nation's services to the sick to a new Department of Health and Community Care. A Labour government will do all of that. We owe it to the sick, and as a society we most certainly owe it to those who care for them.

EUROPE'S ENVIRONMENT TARGETS

The government's desertion of their promise to introduce community care is sadly, far from unique. Indeed, it is the stock-in-trade of the government, especially when they have given undertakings to support social progress or to improve the quality of life and eventually find themselves faced with the demand to deliver. They have a Prime Minister who used to present herself as the guardian of the earth. They have a Secretary of State for the Environment, who I thought at one time was so green that he was inhaling carbon dioxide and exhaling oxygen. The Tories have had eleven years in power, huge resources and inexhaustible supplies of high quality information and advice on every part of the battle to save the national and global environment. But last week they drew themselves up to their full height and produced an environment White Paper which has something to say about practically everything and something to do about practically nothing at all.

They are not a pressure group; they are not an opposition; they are not a think tank. They are a government that has been in power for eleven years and can exercise power. Even while no one with any sense – certainly none of the leading environment groups – thinks that everything can be done at once, it is reasonable to ask that there should be some specific commitments to specific action. Why do they not at the very least go with our European neighbours and act as they have done against global warming, make the commitment to stabilise carbon dioxide emissions by the year 2000 and make substantial cuts in the early years of the next century? That is what we shall be doing.

Why, when traffic congestion and vehicle pollution are the fastest growing threat to our environment, do they not make the commitment to build a high speed rail network to link every part of Britain with the rest of Europe? That is what we shall be doing. Why don't they make the commitment to establish strong, independent agencies to set and secure environmental standards for food, air and water with the health and safety of children as the benchmark for acceptable standards? That is what we shall be doing. Why do they not in a number of other areas such as the trade in toxic waste, the cleaning up of the North Sea and targets for development aid, act as if they really meant it when they said that they were guardians of the earth? We would accept it and support them.

All of what I list are practical, achievable targets. Indeed, they might be regarded as modest for a government that says that it wants to promote the cleaning of the environment 'from the street corner to the stratosphere', but then they will not commit the resources to clean the street corner. If you do it, you get poll tax capped. So it is not really surprising that while they will sign on the dotted line of just about any international environment conventions, they will take little action to honour such conventions in practice. They will make any commitment as long as it does not commit them to anything.

THE END OF THE COLD WAR
In many ways this last year has been the fastest year in history. A year ago when this conference met, Hungary and Poland had just had their first free elections and still faced what they thought would be a journey of some years to full democracy and independence. Czechoslovakia was still ruled by Husak and the dictatorship re-established in 1968. Romania was still ruled by Ceausescu's barbarism. In East Germany the people were just starting to come out onto the streets, but Honecker was still in power and the Stasi in authority. The Warsaw Pact, so far as anyone knew, was still a cohesive military alliance which faced NATO. The Western Alliance was still confined to its 45-year-old military role. Now here we are in October 1990. Poland and Hungary are independent. Czechoslovakia is a free country under –

glory of glory – the presidency of a playwright. Romania has freedom, but it seems it has yet to achieve the same confident liberty of Czechoslovakia. The Warsaw Pact has effectively ceased to exist. NATO has considered specific proposals for increasing its political role and has resolved upon the establishment of the Conference on Security and Co-operation in Europe in a permanent institution. At midnight tonight there will be no more East Germany or West Germany. That country will be united as a parliamentary democracy. We send from here through the West German ambassador – from tomorrow, I hope, the German ambassador – Herr von Richthofen, who is here this afternoon, our best wishes and solidarity to the people of Germany for a great and prosperous future in freedom.

These marvellous changes bring of course their own problems and dangers; but they are capable of being surmounted. These changes, which some of us thought to be a very desirable though very distant prospect and many more thought to be utterly inconceivable, are now a reality. The impossible has become possible. Hope has become fact.

On both sides of what was the East-West divide, people who had become resigned to the idea of no change have become impatient for more change. The end of the Cold War has opened the possibility for the first time in history that by negotiation, by verification, by co-operation in a new security community, all prospect of war can be banished from Europe, the continent that has been the bloodiest battlefield of all human history. Because for decades the East–West deadlock has dominated the political shape of the world, the changes being made across this continent make wider and greater change possible across the rest of the world. The task – the hope – of building a new world order, so long the mission of idealists out of power, has now become the frankly and publicly stated objective of those who hold superpower. That is the great change of our age. That is why it is bliss to be alive now, when the possibilities of these great alterations in the fate of humankind are opening up.

IRAQ'S INVASION OF KUWAIT

By great irony, the conditions which produced the declarations of purpose to work for that new world order by the Presidents of the United States of America and the USSR came as a result of military aggression by a tyrant. The invasion and occupation of Kuwait by Saddam Hussein has nothing to commend it, obviously. But in the reaction to it, the community of nations has quickly formed bonds and taken joint action in a way that would have been unthinkable two years ago, or even a year ago. God knows what would have happened in those circumstances, without that possibility of immediate and strong international solidarity against such aggression.

The action taken, firm and universal sanctions and the deployment of force in defence of Saudi Arabia and its neighbours, was absolutely correct. There is no possibility of an aggressor with the nature of Saddam Hussein being prevented from further attempts at conquest by any other means. That is why the action taken has won and kept the active consent of the world community in the United Nations. The scale and solidarity of that consent clearly means that the longest possible time must be given for sanctions to be used to secure the submission of Saddam Hussein to the will of the United Nations. The pressure must be sustained. It must be made clear to the Iraqi dictator that not only does he not have any friends anywhere now, but he can look forward to no accommodation from any part of the world unless and until he withdraws unconditionally from Kuwiat. The solidarity of nations must continue to be so implacable that even in his Iraqi fortress Saddam Hussein understands that the shutters of the world are up against him and will stay up against him for as long as he illegally occupies another country.

Saddam Hussein must be made to succumb to international law. It must be done in such a way as to deny him the fruits of aggression, the means of further aggression, any gain to reputation, any status of martyrdom. In the course of resolving this crisis, every possible effort must be made to avoid creating the conditions for further and even worse turmoil. If that is not done, then Saddam Hussein could so easily, in the eyes of so many people in the Arab countries, be turned from being an aggressor, so scornful of Arab unity that he attacked the neighbouring Arab country and slaughtered its people, into being the greatest Arab resistance leader of a generation.

The world community, having imposed the rule of law, must then keep the peace. It is an unending obligation, and one that can only be discharged if, in the wake of the withdrawal from Kuwait, there is a firm and sustained embargo on the sale of all weapons and weapons manufacturing machinery to the country of Iraq. It can only be sustained if Iraq's chemical weapons and chemical weapon-making equipment is totally dismantled and if Iraq is thoroughly monitored to establish whether there is any nuclear weapon-making capacity and, if there is, that it be utterly removed and never returned. That is what must happen after Kuwait is cleared.

These purposes can, and must, be fulfilled. But let everyone heed the fact that if they are to be, then the world community must also, first, spread and exert its authority to see that similar actions are taken in the case of other nations with possible chemical and nuclear weapons capacity. Secondly, international action to control and reduce the world arms and arms manufacturing trade will have to be taken with a breadth and thoroughness never previously known in history. We must learn the lesson of where Saddam Hussein got his weapons.

A NEW WORLD ORDER

The whole world now has a vested interest in trying to see that Iraqi withdrawal from Kuwait is achieved, if possible by peaceful means. The reasons for that go far beyond the need to remove any threat to the security of much of the world's oil reserves, important that is to every nation, rich and poor. In the weeks since the United Nations first responded to the Iraqi invasion, it has become clear that there is a real ambition to forge a new and effective structure for world security. If such a structure could be given strength, it would have boundless potential for co-ordinated international action, not just to prevent or push back aggression, but even to combat poverty, to protect the environment and to become an agency, if not for democracy, then at least for recognisable freedom. None of that is certain. None of it is guaranteed. There is no straight path leading from the Security Council and its specific resolutions towards a new, golden age of liberty, prosperity and safety for the whole of the planet. But it is important to know that the objective is now within the realms of possibility and not smothered by Cold War or excluded by hopelessness. Such a development offers a prospect of stable peace unknown in history. It is, in the words of President Bush in Congress very recently, a 'new world struggling to be born'.

No one should found all their hopes – even less all their policies – upon that effort. It could yet be a house built on sand. But what everybody should do is to open up their minds to the possibility that it can be a firmly based and enduring global security structure and that it is worth striving for. The watchword must be 'Don't dream of what may be; work for what can be.' The understanding must be that it is worth working for.

There are countless reasons for that. This afternoon I give you one: children – the children of the earth. Of the world's children under the age of five, 40,000 die every day, mainly from hunger and preventable diseases of hunger. Of the world's children, twenty million suffer severe malnutrition, 150 million are chronically underfed and 100 million children never have any schooling. The statistics of childhood misery and early death in this world are horrifying.

The cause of most of the countries' tragedies is poverty. The poverty is brought about not by natural disasters, but by exploitation, under-development and war. Those evils can be stopped. They are man-made. They can be man-prevented. It is within the power of the adults of the world to do that. That power could be multiplied beyond measure if the structures of security which are now amongst the ambitions of world leaders were established to promote aid, to protect the environment, to relieve debt burdens, to establish fair trade, to spread education, health care and housing in place of ignorance, disease and squalor.

In this party we will not be dreaming of that, we will be working for it. We are democratic socialists. Our cause is the welfare of the community. We recognise no boundaries in that cause between countries or continents. We shall work for the new security structures; we shall work for the new world order, because it is natural to us and necessary for our country and for our world. We shall go on doing it in opposition and we shall do it with full effect in government. That day is coming. We are fit and ready not just to win, but to govern the people of this country. Let us fulfil that purpose, not for our own advantage, but out of our duty to the people of our country and of our world.

1991
BRIGHTON

'It is time for Labour'

Eighteen hours before Kinnock rose to deliver his 1991 conference speech, the news dribbled out that John Major would not, after all, call an autumn general election. There was no official announcement; instead a small group of newspaper journalists had been briefed about the decision, in the hope that it would first become public on the morning of Kinnock's speech and upstage him. Instead, rumours began to circulate in Brighton on the Monday evening. By the late evening television bulletins, the reports had been confirmed.

Instead of upstaging Kinnock, the news gave him a perfect springboard, with the manner of its circulation providing a ready target for his mockery. Kinnock sought to capitalise on the government's propaganda cock-up by echoing his attack on Militant in 1985. Instead of a council 'scuttling round in taxis', we had a government 'scuttling round the press'. In fact, this part of his speech had little impact on Kinnock's immediate audience, which did not seem immediately to detect the echo; Kinnock's more effective jibe, both in the hall and in extracts from his speech played on news bulletins throughout the Tuesday evening, was his retort to ministers: 'You can run but you cannot hide.'

If the cack-handed method of Major's election-timing decision had lifted the immediate tension over the date, that tension had itself come at the end of nine months of opinion poll gyrations. Conservative Party fortunes had started to recover immediately Margaret Thatcher had decided to resign as Prime Minister. From November 1990, when Conservative MPs elected Major as their leader, to March 1991, following the allied victory in the Gulf War, the Tories remained ahead of Labour in the polls. Some Tories believed that Major should have called an election in the early spring of 1991, both to demonstrate that he enjoyed his own mandate, and to capitalise on the twin short-

209

term advantages of a honeymoon with the electorate and his skilful handling of the Gulf crisis. But Major ruled out a 'khaki' election; the wisdom of his decision appeared to be confirmed by the result of the Ribble Valley by-election in March, when the Conservatives lost their fourteenth safest seat to the Liberal Democrats.

Expectations of a June election were dashed by Labour and Liberal victories in the May local elections, followed by a by-election at Monmouth, where Labour overturned a Conservative majority of 9,350. Between mid-May and late-August, Labour held a clear, if modest, poll lead, and there seemed little chance of an election before 1992. But in late August and early September two events combined to alter those calculations. The abortive Soviet coup gave Major the chance to perform as an international statesman; and a rise in consumer confidence appeared to herald an end to recession. A succession of polls put the Tories back in the lead, and speculation about a possible November election swiftly mounted.

However, by the end of September, the Soviet-coup effect had worn off, and consumer confidence had begun to slip once more – and the Conservatives lost their lead over Labour.

Kinnock had prepared his speech as his opening volley of an autumn campaign. The postponement of that campaign came too late for large structural changes; so his speech stands as his prospectus for a Labour government. In sections on the economy, industry, health and taxation, Kinnock sought to develop and refine the combination of caution and radicalism he had offered in earlier speeches.

One new section was added: constitutional reform. Some elements of this – such as devolution, reform of the House of Lords and freedom of information – had been party policy for some years. But in 1991 Labour's policy evolved on two other issues: a bill of rights and electoral reform. Labour had previously been sceptical about having a bill of rights, mainly on the grounds that this would tilt power from elected politicians to unelected judges. However, the experience of twelve years of executive power in the hands of the Conservatives had persuaded many in the Labour Party that some external check on the Government was now desirable.

On electoral reform, Labour's policy review had raised the possibility of using more proportional systems than first-past-the-post for Scotland, Wales and the English regions; for elections to the European Parliament; and for a reformed upper house. A working group had been proposed to explore the options in detail. 1990's conference had decided to extend the remit of the working group, chaired by Professor Raymond Plant of Southampton University, to include elections to the House of Commons. An interim report, containing analysis but no conclusions, was published in July 1991; the final report of the Plant Inquiry was planned for the summer of 1992. Meanwhile, Kinnock took the opportunity of his 1991 speech, and Major's prevarication over the date of the impending general election, to announce that he would abolish the Prime Minister's power to determine the date of dissolution, and move towards a system of fixed-term Parliaments instead.

PK

WHAT A year it has been for the Conservatives! They started it by losing their leader and ended it by losing their nerve. Last night it became evident that Britain has a government that is afraid of the people. I want to tell the Conservative Party this: 'You can postpone people's choice but you will not change the people's verdict. You can run but you cannot hide.'

If I may coin a phrase, what we are seeing is a government, a British government, scuttling round the press handing out rumours through its own ministers. Well, I tell them this, they cannot play politics with people's jobs and people's lives. The people will hold them to account. The Prime Minister cannot even bring himself to make a candid public statement, telling the people that he is running away from their judgment and trying to prolong his fingernail grip on power. It will do him no good; worse, it does this British democracy no good when a government manipulates in this fashion. It must be ended, and Labour will end such a system.

The people of Britain want a government that puts the country first, not the party first and they will get that with a Labour government, for that is what this party wants. It wants our country rebuilt again, our country bold, audacious and just again. We will put the country first. We are ready, fit to serve and able to lead Britain to a better future. We have the policies that the people want. We have a fine team for government, indeed we have the best team for government, of that there is no doubt and we have been building support in every contest.

In this last year we have continued our successes in local government elections. There are now more Labour councillors and more Labour councils in Britain than there ever have been in history. We have continued our successes in Parliamentary by-elections and particularly in that spectacular victory in Monmouth and in that

212

unique contest in Walton. Militant, squeezed into the open, were soundly beaten by democratic socialists, and they always will be beaten by democratic socialists.

Comrades, we have earned our support and we shall earn our victory by addressing the real needs of the people of our country. By looking at a future instead of reaching for the past, by being positive. The Tories have done the opposite. They fought the European elections in 1989 relying entirely on negatives and name calling. They lost. In the local elections last year and this year they relied on negatives and name calling. They lost. They will be relying on negatives and name calling again in the General Election and they will lose again. As my father used to say: 'The best answer to dirty play, boy, is score a goal.' We are going to score a goal.

Comrades, one of the main reasons why they will lose and deserve to lose, is that they are stale and sour. They have no fresh directions, no fresh approaches to offer to the British people. After years in which the Tories have put Britain at the bottom of the league for growth, bottom of the league for investments, bottom of the league for jobs, they still have no policies for building and keeping strong economic recovery. With one million people on hospital waiting lists, 150,000 homeless families and the highest recorded crime rate in British history, they still have no policies to make our country more fair, more secure. After twelve wasted years, if you want to see their monuments, look around you. Even worse, if you want to see their future, look around you. It is clear from everything they say and everything that they do that a fourth term of Tory government would mean more of the same. A fourth term of Tory government would mean at least two more years of poll tax, the tax which could be, should be – and when we are elected will be – abolished immediately.

A fourth term of Tory government would mean years more of under-funding for schools and under-investment for training. It would mean years more of moving the National Health Service into the market. More years of Toryism would mean years more of falling behind our neighbours and competitors in Europe. It would mean years more on the recession roundabout. If the Tories kept power their policies would again take our country through the rise in credit finance consumption, the rise in deficits, the rise in debt, in inflation, in interest rates and then bring the return to recession and rising unemployment all over again. We know that would happen because they are doing now, in their second recession, exactly what they did in their first recession and by following the same policies they would get the same result, a third recession.

The Tories are a government in blinkers, hoping that the British people are wearing blindfolds. They hope in vain. People see what is happening in their own country. They live with the realities and the people of Britain want fresh direction, they want new approaches. People look at the state of our economy, 1,000 businesses a week going bankrupt, 3,000 people losing their jobs every week, redundancies, closures, in the south as well as the north, the east and the west, in high tech industry, in high street shops, they see all that and they live with all that and they say: 'It has to change.' People look at the state of our society and they look at our neighbours in the rest of the European Community. They see the high standards of training, the quality of child care, the investment in public transport and they ask: 'Why not here, why not here in Britain?'

CREATING A MODERN ECONOMY

The answer is, it can change, we can do it here with a Labour government and I say that with certainty because we shall be doing here in Britain what others have done and are doing in more successful economies. We shall be investing in economic strength as others do and we shall be providing a climate for investment as others do. That is the foundation of the standards of living and the continuing economic vitality in other Community countries. Their provision for pensioners, for training, for child care, for education and transport and health does not come out of huge levels of taxation. It does not come out of higher levels of public expenditure. It comes from sustained economic success. Success that has been built because year on year they have invested more in their people, invested more in their economy. They have planted wealth to grow wealth. That is what we must do. Those governments, socialist, conservative, coalition governments, whatever else separates them, share a sense of responsibility. They know it is the prime duty of any modern government, certainly any modern democratic government, to create conditions for business to succeed and for individuals and communities to thrive.

Britain needs a government with a sense of purpose that will provide the country with a new sense of direction. That is the way for Britain to catch up, to compete, to give of its best and to get the best.

We will form such a government and our purpose in government will be to help to create a modern industrial economy so that the whole of the country is mobilised to gain and to maintain prosperity.

We will help to create a modern industrial economy, to compete and to succeed in the single market of the European Community. We will invest just as our competitors do, year on year, continually, strategically. That is the way, not just to help Britain out of recession in the short term, it is the way to enable Britain to stay out of recession in the long term. We will do that with practical policies. We will be providing tax incentives to companies so that they bring forward new investments in plant and machinery. We will begin a phased release of the £6 billion held by local authorities that they have got from the sale of council houses. The Tory government forbids them to use that money. We will get on using it to build homes. We will use it to bring the construction industries out of recession. we will modernise our transport system by mobilising private as well as public investment.

Last week the French Railways Corporation, SNCF, issued a bond in the London money market to raise money to invest in the French high speed rail network, but the Tory government will not let British Rail do the same to get investment in British railways. We will change that. If the French can do it for France, we can do it for Britain and we need it in Britain. It is with practical policies like those that we will begin to build sustained strength in the economy, lasting prosperity for our country, and we will be doing more to foster the development of manufacturing industry – still, after all the devastation of the Tory years, responsible for more than 50 per cent of our income from export, still the basis of strength in a service economy.

FROM INVENTION TO INNOVATION

Economic success in the 1990s and in the new century will be built on innovation, on new products and new processes. Economic success will be built on converting scientific inventiveness into competitive industrial production. The Tory government refuses to recognise that. In the last ten years they have cut the share of public support for research and development. The result is that for every public £1 spent in Britain on discovering and developing new technologies for industry, £1.50 is spent in Italy, £2 is spent in France, £2.35 in Germany. There just is not any comparison even though we face the same challenges in a testing world.

After twelve years of this government the Department of Education and Science estimates that by the mid-1990s Britain will be short of 3,000 qualified technology teachers and 2,000 chemistry teachers. Other research forecasts serious shortages of maths and physics teachers. What a way to enter a new phase of the technological age and the same goes, of course, to teachers of modern languages and indeed in many other areas, where the skills and talents and interests of children need the nourishment of qualified teaching.

All of that would be shameful at any time in any advanced country but it is all the worse in Britain, where the capacity to invent has been and still is so very strong. Everybody knows that British scientists invented the first steam engine, the first electric motors, generators and transformers, radio, television, the first jet engine, the first cardiograph, penicillin, the first computer. The list goes on. It is a glorious list. A list worthy of great pride. But what is much more important to our generation than that pride in what is past, is the fact that the genius of scientific inventiveness is still strong in Britain today. The transputer, fibre optics, the catalytic converter, the body scanner, clean coal technologies, liquid crystal display, holograms, microwave technology – just a few of the epoch-making modern achievements of today's British scientists.

These are the sort of discoveries that change the whole way in which things are made across the world. They change and shape our lives, but the tragedy is that so many of those modern products, developed from the brilliance of contemporary British scientists, are not made here. Not made in Britain. They are taken and developed by overseas firms, turned into manufactures made elsewhere and then sold back to us as finished or part-finished goods. Invented in Britain but made abroad. It is resigning the future.

We have got to change that. We have got to do everything possible to ensure that the products invented in Britain are developed in Britain, made in Britain, sold to the markets of the world from Britain. I make that not as any nationalistic argument but I do say that, when we have these remarkable assets of genius we really should be able to convert them into production in the jobs, in the success, in our own country. That is what we should be doing. We should be making, indeed we have to make, Britain into an innovation-driven economy and we will do it.

We will do it with sustained research funding, we will do it with a

Ministry of Science, we will do it by establishing technology trusts modelled on the success in Germany and Japan. We will be linking research in universities and polytechnics with business and industry. An innovation-driven economy needs a tax system and economic policies which promote sustained investment. It needs monopolies and mergers regulations that promote competition and safeguard company programmes of research and development. We shall make those changes. An innovation economy, above all, needs increases in the quality and the quantity of human skills. The most valuable resource of the country, our only truly renewable resource, is the talent and imagination of our people. Fostering those abilities is essential to personal opportunity, personal prosperity and personal liberty and it is vital to national economic, social and cultural well-being.

The present government refuses to face up to that fact. Bribes are offered to opt out. Money is lavished on city technology colleges, league tables are introduced, when what is really needed is not league tables but laboratory equipment, modern classrooms and qualified teachers to work in those classrooms. Kenneth Clarke, saying why he thought he had to have league tables last week, said that what happened inside schools was a mystery. Well, we know why it is a mystery to Kenneth Clarke, he does not use those schools.

I tell you what is the real mystery. It is how a government, in twelve years, collects unprecedented assets, revenues from North Sea oil, the sell-off of public resources, the highest tax bill in British history and still manages to cut expenditure on education by £3 billion. That is a mystery. Why has he been doing all that? Training is cut, research is cut, capital and revenue support for schools is cut, support for colleges is cut. Clearly, our country cannot hope to succeed with such policies.

That is why, as you heard from Jack Straw and Tony Blair yesterday, we have set out and we will implement new directions in education and training. We are going to make proper commitment to primary schools. We are going to improve the National Curriculum so that every student can combine academic and vocational subjects. We are going to make post-sixteen provision that will take us towards the standards achieved elsewhere in the European Community. We are going to develop the higher and adult education system, so that all people who can take advantage of it can do so to bring out the best in themselves, right throughout their lives. Yes, and we will be expanding and improving pre-school education too. That should be basic to any modern society so that children can learn and parents, especially their mothers, can earn.

If anyone does not understand why it is so important, perhaps I can tell you an everyday story by way of explanation. It is the story of a four-year-old child, of a father with an industrial disease which meant that he had to travel long distances for specialist treatment and of a mother with training but without anyone to look after the child because the family was a lengthy bus journey away. What saves that family from living on unemployment benefit? A nursery school. A nursery school with good facilities and qualified teachers ten minutes away from home.

The nursery school that I went to forty-five years ago, the nursery school that meant that my father could get his treatment and then eventually get back to work, the nursery school that meant my mother could return to nursing and serving the community, a nursery school enabling and transforming the lives of a whole family. That is the reason for pre-school education.

That was 1946. Now, in 1991, standards of that kind really should not be too much to ask in a modern country, should they?

In the rest of the European Community, it is taken for granted. 88 per cent of three to five-year-olds in Italy get pre-school education, 95 per cent in Belgium, 95 per cent in France. In Britain just 40 per cent of under-fives get pre-school education and but for the efforts of Labour councils up and down the country, the figure would be a fraction of that. That has got to change and with a Labour government it will change, so that we can reach those European standards and give children and parents in Britain the same chances and the same security.

'AN ODYSSEY OF DELIGHT'

Comrades, incentives to invest, proper commitment to education and training, modern transport, scientific and industrial innovation: these are the new directions that Britain needs to build long-term competitiveness and lasting prosperity. These are the new directions that Britain must take to succeed in the European single market and the movement towards economic and monetary union that lies beyond that. These are the changes that are coming in Europe. We must be ready for them. If we lag, we lose, yet again.

That is why we are determined to put Britain into Europe's first division and we have the policies to do it. That is the basic difference between ourselves and the Tories. We will actively engage in building that productive strength, building the strength of our country and unlike any other government in the European Community, the Tories turn away from that duty.

Of course, when some of the more glib commentators consider our programme – the training, the investment incentives, transport policies – they say it is not exciting, it is not adventurous. Not adventurous! If passengers could be certain to travel on fast, clean trains, have a seat – there is a revelation – and arrive on time, that would be an odyssey of delight, not just an adventure.

Not adventurous, when a British breakthrough in science can find British finance, be developed and turned into production in British factories, using British design teams, creating jobs in Britain and exports for Britain? I think that is quite enthralling. Not adventurous, when a twenty-seven-year-old miner, whose livelihood has collapsed around him because of his redundancy, gets good training, a marketable skill, a job, wages, choices, the confidence of knowing that he can care properly for his family? That is a real adventure.

At the same time, a thirty-five-year-old housewife, who stayed at home and brought up the children, back in the labour market but very unsure of her skills, gets decent training and becomes a qualified technician, with the income, status and opportunity that goes with it. That is a real-life adventure. It transforms people's lives and the result of all of the advances of this kind, multiplied across the nation, would make a well-equipped country, a country that welcomes the adventure of the future because the people have the skills, the industries have the investment, to face the challenges with confidence.

HEALTH AND WELFARE

Confidence, of course, is more than a matter of job opportunities, vital though they are. It is also a matter of security, and security comes in many forms and from many sources. People need the security of knowing, for instance, that the environment in which they live, the water they drink, the food they eat and the air they breath, are all safe. In a complex modern society, in a contaminated world, that safety can only be achieved if governments are active and vigilant, if governments give the people the power to be active and vigilant and if governments and people work together to protect and to improve the global environment. It is for that reason that our environmental policies are centred on government accepting its obligations to protect and promote sustainable development and on citizens being given the right in law to ensure that those obligations are fully met.

Confidence, security, is also a matter of knowing that if things go wrong and they do go wrong for people, it does not mean they plunge into poverty. That is why we will overturn the Tory policies which have spread poverty and dependency to ten million people in Britain, including two and a half million children, one in five of Britain's children in poverty under this government. We are going to work to end child poverty. We will begin immediately by restoring the value of child benefit and we will, of course, also be combating child and family poverty by introducing the national minimum wage.

Confidence and security come from knowing that when people retire they will get a pension that permits them to enjoy life and not just to exist and we will be starting to make that advance by raising pensions by £8 and £5 and making other improvements.

Confidence and security come from knowing that you can rely on a high quality National Health Service, free when you need it, whoever you are, wherever you live. Confidence and security. That security is cherished by the British people. That is why they regard the National Health Service to be their most precious public asset and it is the reason why in the Labour Party we are determined to support it, strengthen it and ensure that it thrives as a people's service.

In stark contrast the Tories want to take the National Health Service to pieces, to hand it over to the market, to make it a creature of contracts and commerce. The difference between us could not be greater. Labour will modernise the National Health Service. The Tories privatise the National Health Service. That is the difference.

Of course they protest that they will not, but that means that they either do not understand or they will not admit to understanding the dynamic of the process that they have already started. Their hospital opt-outs will create, and are intended to create, a health service consisting of trading units. Their GP contract system will create and is intended to create, a market place of haggling doctors, 'buying and selling patients', as the Chairman of the British Medical Association put it. In each case, the ability of private purchasers to buy advantage in a market system – because that is what a market system means – will mean increasing dependence by the NHS on the sale of treatment. That will happen whether patients are buying treatment as a matter of preference or whether they are buying it in desperation as free health care shrinks and the queues get longer. That is the way that the deck is stacked. You diminish the standard by under-funding. You further isolate it by introducing a market system and eventually people who have every faith in the health service and no intention of buying, are goaded by pain and anxiety into becoming customers instead of just being patients.

The process is called privatisation. There are some areas of the health service which a privatised system would not really want, of course. Long-term care of the elderly in hospital. The care of the psychiatrically ill and community care really have not got much of what could be called profitable potential. Accidents and emergencies – well, we have expert testimony there. The managers of the Royal Liverpool University Hospital Trust 'marketing plan' advise that 'emergency admissions are relatively unattractive from a commercial viewpoint'. Yes, that is the plan they put out . Who can want a health service to be run according to judgments like that, a commercial viewpoint?

The doctors, nurses and health workers, they do not want it. The patients and the public do not want it. None of those people, the people who provide the health service, the people who use the health service, they have not demanded the Tory changes. The only demand for these changes has come from a government determined to ram the market system into every corner, every nook and cranny, of national life and of public service and the British people do not want the market system rammed into every corner of the public services.

At the next election the British people will be deciding whether they keep the National Health Service or whether they lose the National Health Service. Those who vote Labour will be voting to build up the NHS. Those who vote otherwise will be voting to break up the National Health Service. Many people, including Conservatives, do not want that but they must be advised that is the true choice and measure their vote accordingly. When people vote Labour, they will be voting to stop the opt-outs, they will be voting to put an end to the cuts and closures. They will be voting for the practical policies of preventative medicine.

When people vote Labour they will be voting for the introduction of a comprehensive system of care in the community, with the funds ring-fenced so that they all go directly to the elderly infirm and the chronically sick and disabled, being cared for in the community. In voting Labour the British people will also be voting to ensure that the full revenues from economic growth are used year on year to meet the needs of the whole nation and not to favour the few. That is Labour's policy and is the people's priority. We know and the nation knows that providing for the treatment of the sick, caring for the old and giving full opportunities to the young must come before any tax cuts.

TAXATION

That is the order of priorities of the British people, the sense of purpose of the British people, but it is an order of priorities and sense of purpose that the Tories have not shown and will never follow. The reductions that they have made in top-rate taxes since 1988 alone have already cost £10 billion. Now they are planning to cut another billion off inheritance tax. A country whose health service has to have raffles and fun runs to buy basic hospital equipment cannot afford giveaways like that to the best-off in our country.

Comrades, all the time it is the people in the middle and the people at the bottom, who pay for the tax cuts for the very few at the top. That is why the tax burden in Britain, the tax burden on the whole country, the tax burden on the average family, is higher than it was in 1979, higher than it has ever been in peace time.

The Tories have always had an open-ended tax system and the open end is spelt VAT. Whenever they have been under pressure they have hoisted VAT. They did it when they came to power, they did it earlier this year, when they plunged into the poll tax crisis and they would do it again if they ever got the chance. That is the Tory way, everybody pays higher tax. We believe that in a civilised society the best-off minority must pay their fair share to meet the needs of the majority. That is not the politics of envy, that is the ethics of immunity, the ethics of society.

It is the course that we choose and the course that the British people want. In following that course we will not be spending what the country cannot afford. We will not borrow for consumption and we will not increase the tax contributions of the huge majority of the people. We think that people pay enough tax already and we also believe that a government that has to work within the limits pledged to the electorate must be a more efficient government. We will pay for better public services by growth and by ending Tory waste. We will pay for better public services by getting better value for public money.

- Value for money, that is what you get when you stop wasting £18 million of tax payers' money every day propping up the poll tax.
- Value for money is what you get when you stop wasting £500 million paying accountants and administrators to privatise the National Health service and not an extra bed to show for it. Value for money, that is what you get when you stop wasting £6 billion of taxpayers' money trying to bribe people out of the State Earnings-Related Pensions Scheme. Value for money, that is what you get when you build homes instead of paying huge bills for bed and breakfast in hostels for the homeless, week in week out, month in month out, year in year out.
- Value for money is what you get when you start to collect the £5 billion in taxes lost every year because of evasion. That is what a value for money government will do. It is what a Labour government will do.

CONSTITUTIONAL REFORM

Discharging the duties of government obviously goes beyond managing the money of the country, vital though that is. For democratic government, it extends to strengthening the democratic powers and rights of the people. We shall do that and we shall do it by decentralising the government and by empowering the people of Britain. We will introduce a freedom of information Act.

We will increase accountability by ensuring that everyone everywhere can vote in elections for part of their council every year. We are going to reform the House of Lords, improve the legal aid system, introduce devolution, first to Scotland and then progressively and with consent to Wales and to the regions of England.

We will enact our Charter of Rights, backed up by a complementary Bill of Rights. We are going to make these and other changes because our party and our people recognise and respond to the need for stronger safeguards for personal and civil rights and responsibilities in Britain.

In making changes we are dealing in a practical and progressive way with the essential questions of how our country is ruled and whether the system of rule serves the changed and changing needs of the nation. These are the actions of a confident and liberating party. A party that believes that the duty of democratic government extends to enabling the people and to giving extra vitality to democracy.

You proved that again in this conference last year when you voted to establish the working party on electoral systems. The decision was taken in recognition of the fact that this is a serious issue of debate, that it must be addressed with the fullest and widest public information and that it is about the basic questions of the quality and strength of representation and government and not about the tactical jostling of parties and politicians. That is what the issue is about. It is the right way to approach democratic change and that is how we will approach it in government.

Comrades, change is most certainly needed. In these last twelve years the centralisation of government power has been intensified. There has been a continual effort to politicise the Civil Service and to subordinate government employees. Local democracy, whether run by Labour, Conservative or anybody else, has been seriously eroded. Political patronage has been used on a prodigious scale. Official secrecy has been increasingly used for the protection of government interest and not for the protection of the public interest.

In these last twelve years women, the majority of our country, have lost rights under the law, not been granted in any way at all an advance to real equality under the law. All that has happened and is happening in a modern country with deep democratic roots. It has not produced efficiency and competence in government. It has produced arrogance, incompetence, shiftiness, waste in government and it has proved that many civil and individual rights which we thought to be basic and unbreakable in Britain have, in reality, been fragile. We need to safeguard against that fragility. That is why in government we will make constitutional change to give new potency to democracy and to promote good government in our democracy. We will strengthen freedom here by adding to it and as we do that we must also nurture the freedom growing elsewhere by actively supporting it.

FOREIGN POLICY
The need to do that and the opportunity to do that increased beyond measure six weeks ago when the drunken conspirators in the Kremlin

were defeated. The world became a different place and it changed for the better again last Friday, when President Bush announced his fresh initiative for disarmament on an unprecedented scale. Britain must be part of that progress. We must be part of the new negotiations on verifiable disarmament and we should be doing everything possible now, straightaway, as a Labour government will, to bring in the other nuclear powers, to halt and reverse proliferation and to secure agreements to end testing of nuclear devices. That is the active role that we should be taking in the world and we have got to be part of the efforts to ensure that progress is sustained in the Soviet Union too.

The course of action that we must take is clear. I offer you this statement as a guide: 'I often hear the question, how can the West help us today? My reply is as paradoxical as the whole of my life has been. You can help us most if you help the Soviet Union on its irreversible but immensely complicated road to democracy.' They are the words of President Havel of Czechoslovakia speaking to the United States Congress last year. Nothing could be more articulate, nothing could be more persuasive about the need to give active support to the development of democracy and change in the Soviet Union and those words of a former victim of Soviet oppression, a great democrat, a man of unsurpassed humanity, Vaclav Havel. We must help to make that advance to democracy and economic security and we must help to ensure that it is stable and peaceful and since disarmament is central to economic progress in the Soviet Union our aid must be linked to that. As Oleg made clear on this platform on Monday, that is what the democrats of the Soviet Union and its Republics want us to do and we must not let them down.

Our help will feed the roots of freedom and just as it will contribute to the economic and political security of the people of the Soviet Union and its former satellites, so it will be an investment in our own well-being. As the massive resources that have been dedicated to the Soviet military system are diverted to civil production, we in the West can increase our peace dividend. We must use it to build economic strength. We must use it as an industrial dividend, a production dividend, a job dividend, an investment dividend, so that any peace dividend that we get in our generation is an enduring source of wealth and not merely a short-term bonus that has to be used for paying redundancy and unemployment benefits. We can make it that source of continual wealth for expenditure on the social priorities and the development of our country, if we use that dividend properly for the purpose of investment to advance our economy.

We certainly need that economic strength in Britain. We need it for Britain and we need it in order to help to combat poverty in a world in which a silent emergency of starvation is killing countless thousands of children and women and men every week. Nothing, not even the historic changes in Eastern Europe and the potential for famine and turmoil in the Soviet Union, nothing must be allowed to obscure the suffering of the countless destitute millions in Africa, Asia and Latin America.

To those who will not concern themselves with those tragedies, I simply say, if mercy does not move you then concern yourselves with the condition of humanity for your own sake. The misery of the poor today could, in this interdependent world, become your cataclysm tomorrow. Unless the free and affluent countries play their full part in the conquest of poverty, that poverty will eat away at prosperity, security, stability, even liberty itself. We are democratic socialists. In our own society we know that the rights of the individual depend upon the actions of the community. The actions to establish and maintain the political, economic and social freedom. The same is true of the world.

Just as in our own society we know that opportunity for the individual depends upon the way that the community acts together, so we know that is true for the whole world and that is why we say, act together to combat poverty, for in doing so we add to the wealth of all. Act together to defeat ignorance, for in doing so we add to the knowledge of all. Act together to cure and prevent disease, for in doing so we promote the health of all. Act together to protect the environment, for in doing so we all become safer. Act together to stop war, for in doing so we all profit from peace. Act together as a world, one humanity.

CONCLUSION

Friends, in our country and for the sake of our country, it is time for a new direction, time for a government with a sense of real national purpose. As we approach the year 2000, we the British people have to decide how we are going to mark the end of the millennium and the beginning of a new age. Is it to be with nothing much more than a New Year's Eve party? Are we going to be able to greet the year 2000 as a fair and free society, a strong and productive economy, a confident and creative people? If that is the future that we want and it is, it must be prepared for with determination, vitality, vision. Only we will do that. Conservatives never will. The democratic socialism that we believe in is, above all, about enabling people to get the best out of life by putting the best into life. Its purpose is to ensure that people are prepared for the future, able to control their own destiny. Conservatism, especially British Toryism, is above all about letting the future look after itself, about letting people fend for themselves, whether they are able to or not.

Now is the time for change from their way. Time to build Britain's industrial strength, time to make our National Health Service modern and secure, time to raise the standards of our skills and schools, time to create a cleaner, safer environment. It is time to start transforming Britain from the country it has become to the country we know it can be. It is time for that change. It is time for Labour.